The Interior Life of St. Thomas Aquinas

Christ: "You have written well of Me, Thomas; what reward do you wish for your labors?" Thomas: "Nothing less than You, O Lord!"

The INTERIOR LIFE *of* ST. THOMAS AQUINAS

by

Dr. Martin Grabmann,
Prothonotary Apostolic, Professor of Theology at the University of Munich

Translated by Nicholas Ashenbrener, O.P., Dominican House of Studies, River Forest, Illinois

SOPHIA INSTITUTE PRESS
Manchester, New Hampshire

Originally published in 1951 by the Bruce Publishing Company, Milwaukee, WI.

Cover by Updatefordesign Studio.

Cover image: *St. Thomas Aquinas* by Juan de Peñalosa y Sandoval and Thomas, On Books about Generation and Corruption (Picryl 4733257 00007).

Frontispiece: S. Thomas d'Aquin, March 7th, from "Les Images De Tous Les Saincts et Saintes de L'Année" (Metropolitan Museum of Art).

Nihil Obstat: Fr. J. S. Considine, O.P., S.T.M.: Fr. J. W. Curran, O.P., B.S.T., S.T.D.

Imprimi Potest: Fr. Eduardus L. Hughes, O.P., S.T.Lr., Chicagiensi, Ill., die 15a Aprilis, 1951

Nihil Obstat: John A. Schulien, S.T.D., *Censor Librorum*

Imprimatur: ✠ Moyses E. Kiley, Archiepiscopus Milwaukiensis die 1a Maii, 1951

Sophia Institute Press
Box 5284, Manchester, NH 03108
1-800-888-9344
www.SophiaInstitute.com

Library of Congress Cataloging-in-Publication Data

Names: Grabmann, Martin, 1875-1949 author. | Ashenbrener, Nicholas, translator.

Title: The interior life of St.Thomas Aquinas / by Dr. Martin Grabmann, Prothonotary Apostolic, Professor of Theology at the University of Munich; translated by Nicholas Ashenbrener, O.P., Dominican House of Studies, River Forest, Illinois.

Other titles: Das Seelenleben des heiligen Thomas von Aquin. English

Identifiers: LCCN 2023043338 (print) | LCCN 2023043339 (ebook) | ISBN 9798889110927 (paperback) | ISBN 9798889110934 (ebook)

Subjects: LCSH: Thomas, Aquinas, Saint, 1225?-1274.

Classification: LCC BX4700.T6 G67313 2024 (print) | LCC BX4700.T6 (ebook) | DDC 282.092--dc23/eng/20231220 LC record available at https://lccn.loc.gov/2023043338 LC ebook record available at https://lccn.loc.gov/2023043339

First printing

Contents

Translator's Preface

WHILE PREPARING THE TRANSLATION of this book during the early days of 1949, news reached me of the sudden death of its author, the late Msgr. Martin Grabmann. The passing of such a champion of truth is indeed a great loss to Thomistic scholarship.

His staggering number of publications, begun as early as 1898, clearly manifested a profound student and ardent admirer of the Angelic Doctor. Not only did he grasp the precise thought of St. Thomas, but he very clearly understood the whole historical background of the Middle Ages that helped to fashion the Prince of Theologians. Because of his extensive knowledge, the name of Dr. Martin Grabmann today represents a foremost authority on the life, works, and interpretation of St. Thomas Aquinas.

Practically all of Dr. Grabmann's writings lie hidden in some foreign language. Many of them would be of inestimable profit to the English-speaking public. This particular work was selected in preference to his many other works for good reasons. Today, with the ever-increasing desire for the sound doctrine of St. Thomas, there is a dire need for a work in English on the spiritual life of this learned Doctor. Many recent writers have done beautiful sketches of Thomas the Doctor, but few, if any, have succeeded as Grabmann has in portraying Thomas the saint.

This little work is also singular in its revelation of the sanctity and holiness of the author's priestly soul. And so it becomes especially fitting that this translation be dedicated to him in memory of his love for God and truth. It is a work that always remained close to his heart. Such can be evidenced in the brief eulogy penned by his close friend, the editor of *Divus Thomas*, G. M. Häfele, O.P.* The last paragraph reads:

> He (Grabmann) set his heart for immortality … principally on one little book: *Das Seelenleben des heiligen Thomas von Aquin.* After the

* G. M. Häfele, O.P., "Protonotar Dr. Martin Grabmann. In Piam Memoriam," *Divus Thomas*, März, 1949, Paulus-Druckerie, Freiburg in der Schweiz.

> first two editions were sold out, he waited until the last days of his life to see its reappearance. . . . Today we place this work upon his freshly-dug grave not only as a modest token of our grateful love and loyalty for our paternal friend but also as an eloquent testimony of how deeply he penetrated into the thought and the inner life of the Angelic Doctor, and of how well he realized and fulfilled the request of the Church in its prayer for the feast of St. Thomas Aquinas: "both clearly to understand the things he taught, and faithfully to imitate what he did."

Within this translator's preface, I am also including some thoughts that the author has placed in his brief preface. This will eliminate the necessity of having two prefaces to this short work. Besides, some of Dr. Grabmann's reflections would have little or no interest for an English-speaking audience.

This work, as the author points out, originated from lectures that he delivered in various German cities on the occasion of the sixth centennial of St. Thomas's canonization, celebrated in 1923. It appeared in two editions published by the *Theatinerverlag.* Sometime after all available copies had been exhausted, the *Paulusverlag* took up the work, had it brought up to date by its author, and republished it in 1949. The English translation has been made from this third and enlarged revision.

Throughout the translation, I have scrupulously tried to remain as close as possible to the original, knowing that it breathed the spirit of peace and quiet of a soul similar to St. Thomas. The only changes that have been introduced have been those of grammar, or in peculiar constructions where the English version would, of necessity, differ from the German. All quotations have been rechecked and, when more suited, translated from the original. All omissions within quotations have been clearly indicated wherever it seemed the German did not include some thought or phrase. Much of the Latin phraseology has been put into English so as to make the work more accessible to an English-speaking audience. Wherever the Latin had to be retained, its meaning can easily be discerned from either the context or the translation that immediately follows. Since the footnotes, in large part, only indicate the sources, and these are usually in some foreign language, they have been relegated to an appendix in the back of the book. Thus the work should become more presentable and readable in its new English garb.

This book is neither a purely devotional nor a strictly scientific treatment of the interior life of St. Thomas. Rather, it is a happy combination of the two, as only a man like Dr. Grabmann, with his deep insight and extensive experience, can present it. The work is intended, as the author points out, to help acquaint priests, students of theology, and the laity interested in St. Thomas with the religious personality and character of the Angelic Doctor. Those who are intimately acquainted with Thomas should profit by seeing more clearly the *true source* of Thomas's knowledge. Those who have heard or read little of Thomas should profit in discovering the *loving soul* of this master of Catholic thought. All, then, will understand how and why Thomas the saint learned more from the feet of the Crucified than from the innumerable books he read. And they will be convinced that sanctity precedes science, that life precedes knowledge, even in the scientific personality of St. Thomas Aquinas.

In making this translation, I am indebted to our Provincial, the Very Reverend Edward L. Hughes, O.P., for his encouragement and permission to undertake this translation; to Christopher Kiesling, O.P., without whose generous assistance this translation would never have been completed; to Richard Butler, O.P., for his kind help in preparing the English manuscript; and to all those who have aided in many little ways to make this much-needed work find its way into the English language. May all, by immersing themselves into this saintly soul, feel more drawn to the loving personality and living thought of St. Thomas Aquinas, Doctor of the Church and patron of Catholic Schools. This is the prayerful hope both of the author and the translator.

—Nicholas Ashenbrenner, O.P.
Dominican House of Studies
River Forest, Illinois
Feast of St. Thomas,
March 7, 1951

The Interior Life of St. Thomas Aquinas

Introduction

Sometime after the middle of the fourteenth century, the Italian painter Tommaso da Modena[1] adorned the chapter room of San Niccolò, the Dominican convent at Treviso, with frescoes of Dominican saints and scholars. Here, St. Thomas Aquinas is represented standing at the lecturer's chair in front of his desk. He holds a book in his right hand, while his left hand rests upon a tiny church. From a sun gleaming on his breast, stream rays of light that fall upon and enter the church.

This representation of the most learned of the saints and the most saintly of the learned, as Cardinal Bessarion has called Aquinas, is also found in various other places. At Viterbo, on a terra-cotta relief of Andrea della Robbia, the saint holds a book in his left hand, and with his right hand, he sustains another small church. Rays of light shine on the church from a sun set upon his breast. At both sides, angels bow in deepest awe. This same idea is brought out in miniature on some manuscripts, as for instance upon one originally written at St. Domenico's in Fiesole, now at the Biblioteca Medicea Laurenziana in Florence.[2]

In this portrayal of St. Thomas, I see a significant indication of his providential influence within the Church and for the Church over a period of more than six hundred years. He is diffusing rays of light upon the Church, the Church upon which he in return depends—light rays of natural and supernatural truth, rays of warmth for a life of Christian asceticism and mysticism, of supernatural love and perfection. A manuscript, written not long after his death, truly sounds like a prophecy when it says in sacred memory of Brother Thomas: "*cujus doctrina illuminatur sancta ecclesia*" (by whose doctrine Holy Mother Church is illumined).[3]

The rays of light with which St. Thomas illumines the Church in these pictures emanate from a sun fixed upon his breast. In truth, his tremendous influence throughout centuries of Church history springs from his inner life: from the sanctity and purity of his thought, love, and life. We cannot understand the thought and influence of St. Thomas, everywhere diffusing truth, unless we cast a glance into his inner life, into the very life of his soul.

On a fresco at Treviso, underneath the picture of the saint, we read: "*Fuit exemplar virtutum, virgo, eximius magister in sacra theologia, in toto orbe famosus. Multa opera fecit et in multis claruit miraculis.*" (He was a model of virtues, a virgin, a distinguished master in sacred theology, renowned throughout the world. He wrote many works, and worked many miracles.) Here the sanctity and spotless purity of his life precede his scholarly greatness. And Pope Pius XI, in his profound and well-received encyclical *Studiorum Ducem*, commemorating the sixth centenary of St. Thomas's canonization, begins with a most impressive description of his life of virtue.[4]

The following pages are intended to be an analysis, in a simple and plain manner, of his interior life, a sketch of his soul and character. I am presenting this portrait precisely as many years of heartfelt and intimate intellectual familiarity with the work, personality, and thought of St. Thomas have shown and revealed it to me.

If love, occasionally manifesting itself in some colorful tinge, has perchance directed my hand in planning and drawing this portrait, such is not the expression of a momentary enthusiasm and mood that so often mars and tarnishes the reality and impartiality of a representation. Whatever is mentioned here concerning the greatness of St. Thomas, his inner motives and nature, is not intended to be a panegyric.

It is rather simply the impression and expression of whatever an exhaustive study of sources has revealed to me about this great thinker, whom I have learned to love and venerate more and more over the course of years as a holy, pure, and noble personality. Or it arises from whatever glimmers through his works, impersonal as they may seem, about his own interior, personal individuality.

Biographers of St. Thomas have frequently sketched the portrait of the soul and character of our saint. Touron has done this most thoroughly and in greatest detail. He dedicated to this purpose the whole fourth book of his huge biography of St. Thomas, which he wrote from a comprehensive knowledge of sources, as well as of Thomistic works.[5] More recently, enthusiastic and faithful students of St. Thomas have felt their way into his interior life, giving us a description and appraisal of his intellectual and religious personality. The centenary of the canonization of Aquinas, which occasioned many valuable and far-reaching scientific works, partly historical and partly speculative, strongly stimulated a penetration into the interior life of this great theologian and philosopher. Among the contributions called forth by this jubilee, we should mention the works from the pens of the Dominicans M. Gillet, H. Petitot, S. Ramirez, and G.M. Manser.[6] The excellent periodical *La Vie Spirituelle* has published a special section entitled “Saint Thomas Docteur mystique.”

Two Dominicans, A.G. Sertillanges and J. Webert, have sketched very impressive portraits of the scientific and religious greatness of St. Thomas. T. DeMan, O.P., and the Hollander J.E. Kuiper have described his sanctity. Giulio Salvadori, the professor at the Università Cattolica del Sacro Cuore in Milan whose process of beatification has been introduced, has drawn a charming miniature of the inner life of our saint. One reads J. Pieper’s book on St. Thomas Aquinas with a great deal of satisfaction, for it is so expressive of his interior life. Angelus Walz, O.P., has embodied a chapter, “El Santo Dottore,” into his excellent biography of St. Thomas based on a thorough knowledge of sources and data, which presents the life of the Angelic Doctor against the background of contemporary history. I, too, have brought out the scholarly individuality of Aquinas in my work on St. Thomas Aquinas, which has been translated into numerous foreign languages and now has made its appearance in a seventh edition.[7]

CHAPTER 1

Features of the Soul and Character of St. Thomas from His Writings and the Acts of His Canonization

THE ACTS OF THE canonization process and the writings of the saint are the principal sources for our portrait of the soul and character of St. Thomas.[8] A number of testimonies, handed down to us in the acts of the canonization process, depict with great uniformity the foremost features of the inner life and the whole personality of Aquinas.

These testimonies are valuable because either they come from those who have personally known the saint or they are from correspondence between his intimate friends.[9] Among such friends were: first and foremost, Reginald of Piperno, an inseparable companion who knew all the secrets and the inner experiences of the saint—the *socius carissimus*, as St. Thomas calls him; John of Cajatia, another Dominican, who was a student of the Angelic Doctor in Paris and Naples, who had always been especially close to him; William of Tocco, one of the witnesses, who played a very active role in the promotion of his canonization process, and wrote the first Life of St. Thomas upon which the biographies of Bernard Guido and Peter Calo largely depend.

These biographies of St. Thomas are not such living and impressive portraits of a soul as we meet in Eadem's graphic life of St. Anselm of Canterbury or in St. Bonaventure's biography of St. Francis. Even the writings of St. Thomas, in their rigidly scientific arrangement and their abstract, theoretical nature, appear at first glance to offer very little, if anything, for a sketch of his soul and character. The scholastics of the twelfth century, an Anselm of Canterbury, a John of Salisbury, more or less reveal to us their thoughts, wishes, and feelings through their correspondence. Among the great scholastic thinkers who ascended to a leading public position, such as Bonaventure, the General and great organizer of the Franciscan Order, personal motives are naturally interwoven into their literary work. Even St. Albert the Great purposely uses his personal experiences here and there in his writings.

From Thomas himself, we have only one letter, in substance a scientific opinion, written to Abbot Bernard Ayglerius of Monte Cassino—the last work to come from the pen of the saint.[10] Only at the beginning or end of his opuscula, which he wrote at the request of his Dominican brethren and of others seeking advice, do we find some personal turn that offers a glimpse into the pure, noble, and gracious soul of the saint.

Concluding his opinion on the form of absolution, written in accordance with the wish of his Master General, John of Vercelli, St. Thomas writes: "It has been the will of God that I should labor at your command on the feast of the Chair of Peter, writing this work for the defense of the power given to Peter."[11]

Beginning another opusculum, *Responsio de VI articulis ad lectorum Bisuntinum,* Thomas charitably writes: "To my dearest Brother in Christ, Gerard Bisuntinus, of the Order of Friars Preachers, I, Brother Thomas Aquinas of the same Order, send my greetings in fraternal charity. I have received your letters containing some articles, to which you ask me to reply. And although I have been busy with many things, nevertheless, lest I should fail the request of your charity, I took care to answer you as soon as the opportunity permitted."

The saint, entirely engrossed as he was in his many and great labors, must have made sacrifices to answer such questions. Yet, his cordial and sincere charity willingly accepted these interruptions. At the close of this opusculum, he asks Brother Gerard to remember him in his prayers: "These things, very dear Brother, occur to me at this time in answer to the questions which you proposed. For this work, if it pleases you, remember me in your prayers."

In the *Responsio de articulis XXXVI ad lectorem Venetum*,[12] Thomas answers in the same friendly and gracious manner the questions of another one of his brethren: "Having read your letters, I found in them a great number of articles which your charity requested me to answer within four days. And, although I have been very busy, I have put aside for a time the things that I should do and have decided to answer individually the questions which you proposed, so as not to be lacking to the request of your charity."

Apparently, the lector from Venice knew well the self-sacrificing willingness of the saint and therefore demanded the answer to these thirty-six obscure and general questions within four days. In the concluding words, the saint tactfully mentions this want of a clearer formulation: "These are the things, very dear Brother, which I write more elaborately than you requested in response to the articles which you sent. It is not possible to reply absolutely to these opinions for they can be taken in different senses, especially since you have not mentioned what may be objected against these articles. In such a case, a more absolute and certain reply could have been given. May your charity endure, and for this work, please remember me in your prayers." I wonder whether many scholars, famous and overburdened with work, would reply as charitably as Thomas did to the obscure and incomplete requests of a beginner, who sought answers for thirty-six questions within four days!

The saint's devout and religious manner of thinking also manifests itself in the personal remarks of his opuscula. The opusculum, *De substantiis separatis seu de angelorum natura*, dedicated to Reginald of Piperno (*ad fratrem Reginaldum socium suum carissimum*), has the following beautiful words of introduction: "Since we cannot be present at the sacred solemnities of the angels, we should not allow the time of devotion to pass in idleness. But, rather, the time taken away from chanting the office should be given over to the work of writing." The saint here speaks of the regular choral office (*solemnia Angelorum*) carried out in his Order according to a beautiful liturgical rite. He wishes to occupy the time in which he is unable to take part in the regular choral office with the writing of a tract about the angels, one of his most profound speculative treatises.

In the same friendly and charitable way, Thomas also replied to persons outside his Order who came to him seeking counsel and help. A duchess, most likely the Duchess Adelaide of Burgundy (1261–1267), came to the saint with a number of questions concerning her duties of government. He responded to these questions in an extensive work, *De Regimine Judaeorum*.[13] He prefaces the following personal introduction to the factual discussion:

> I have received the letters of Your Excellency (*Excellentiae Vestrae*), from which I fully understand your pious solicitude for the ruling of your subjects, and the devout love which you have for the brethren of our Order. I give thanks to God who has planted in your heart the seeds of such virtues. It has been difficult for me to answer the articles which you requested in your letter, both because of the labors which the duty of lecturing requires, and because I would be pleased if you would seek the advice of others more learned in these affairs. In truth, since I thought it unbecoming to be found a negligent helper, considering your solicitude, or ungrateful, considering your esteem, I have taken care at present to reply to the articles which you proposed, without, however, prejudice to a better opinion.

The concluding words show the same modesty: "At this time it occurred to me, illustrious and pious Lady, that these things should be written in reply to your questions. In these matters I do not so force my own opinion upon you that I do not urge you to hold that of a more learned man."

A noble lay friend, a Lord of Burgo, came to Thomas with a question of moral theology concerning superstitious games of chance. The saint readily instructs him in his *De Sortibus.* The completely lovable character of the saint is mirrored in the introduction: "Your charity has asked me to reply in writing about considerations of games of chance. It is not proper that the requests, which charity faithfully offers, be refused by a friend. So, desiring to satisfy your petition and interrupting my labors of study for a short time during the major vacation, I have considered what must, according to my opinion, be written of games of chance."

Thomas begins his commentary to the *Perihermeneias* with the following dedication:

> To the beloved Superior of Louvain, I, Brother Thomas Aquinas, send greetings and an increase in true wisdom. Moved by the consideration of your diligence, by which you in your youth seek wisdom and not vanity, I have sought, among the many pressing duties of my labors, to prepare a commentary on the book of Aristotle called *Perihermeneias,* which is filled with many obscurities. My intention is to offer the advanced higher things, and yet not to refuse beginners the means of acquiring proficiency. May your zeal, therefore, receive

> the work of the present exposition. If you profit by it, may you inspire me to yet greater efforts.

Let us now proceed to examine in the testimonies of his canonization process the features of the soul and character of St. Thomas. The writings of the saint will then help us to understand these traits and to create a unified portrait.

The Dominican James of Cajatia has given his oath to the following accounts: "I have known Brother Thomas to be a contemplative man (*hominem contemplativum*), totally withdrawn from worldly things and drawn to divine things. He was very honest, pure, and serious. Never did he seek special food, but was content with whatever was placed before him, using it moderately. Every day he celebrated Mass and heard another one. Then, without delay, he devoted himself to prayer, study, and writing." When asked where he had seen Thomas, James replied: "At Naples and Capua in the convents of the Friars Preachers."[14]

The testimony of the Dominican Peter of St. Felix is more detailed. Under oath, he gave the following description of the life and conduct of St. Thomas:

> Brother Thomas was a man of great purity in regard to self as well as in regard to others, for he wished that others should be as he himself

> was. He possessed an admirable humility and patience so that he never saddened anybody by proud or injurious words. He was, moreover, a man of profound contemplation, who constantly either prayed, wrote, or studied. Every day he celebrated Holy Mass and heard another. He was totally removed from earthly affairs to things divine. Never did he seek special food, but was satisfied with what was set before him. Even at table he was often wrapt in contemplation, so that someone could remove the food before him without his knowing it. He also had very little concern about clothing.

Asked how he knew all this, Peter of St. Felix replied: "I myself have seen him, have been his student, and have lived with him in the Order for one year. I have seen him in his cell in the Convent at Naples, in the choir of the church, and in the lecture-hall teaching and preaching."[15]

Conrad of Suess, an elderly priest of the Order of Preachers, revealed under oath his personal impressions of the pure and holy life of Thomas: "Thomas was a man of a holy life and noble disposition. He was peaceful, sober, humble, quiet, devout, contemplative, and so chaste that he was considered a virgin. In food and in drink he practiced such moderation that he never desired any special food, nor was he overly concerned about his apparel. Every day he either celebrated Mass with great devotion, or attended one or two. Except for the hours spent in necessary repose, he continually devoted himself to lecturing, writing, praying, or preaching."[16]

The sworn testimony of William of Tocco is likewise based upon personal acquaintance, although not as intimate. He was prior of the Dominican Convent at Benevento. He was very active in the process of canonization, having been a commissioner from the year 1317. The results of his investigations he condensed into a biography of St. Thomas. He became acquainted with Thomas at Naples near the close of the saint's life when he heard him preach and lecture and noticed how throngs of people crowded about him with devotion to hear his sermons. He continued: "Thomas was a most lovable man (*homo dulcis*), despising temporal honors, so pure and chaste that he was commonly thought to be a virgin as from his mother's womb."

For his testimony, William of Tocco, who was not as intimate with Thomas as the witnesses previously quoted, relied upon those who were better acquainted with him. First, he relied upon Peter of Sectia, who was procurator of the Dominicans in England and preached at Brother Thomas's funeral. In his eulogy, Peter mentioned: "When Thomas was approaching death, he heard his general confession. His whole life was nothing but prayer, contemplation, lectures, sermons, disputations, writings, and dictations."

William of Tocco, who likewise relied upon the information that he had personally received from Reginald of Piperno about the learning of the saint, revealed:

> Thomas did not acquire his knowledge by natural ingenuity, but rather through the revelation and infusion of the Holy Spirit, for he never began to write without previous prayer and tears. Whenever a doubt arose, he had recourse to prayer. After shedding many tears, he would return to his work, now enlightened and instructed.

Brother Reginald gave this and other testimony to William of Tocco in his public lectures.[17]

The sworn accounts of John Regina of Naples, O.P., one of the greatest theologians of the oldest Italian Thomistic School[18] and also an active participant in the canonization process, are based upon those who had a more personal knowledge of Thomas. For the canonization, he prepared a sermon that he was not able to deliver because of sickness. Substantially, his testimony painted the very same picture as the others.[19]

Finally, a valuable testimony from the lips of a man who did not belong to the Dominican Order should be cited. He was Bartholomew of Capua, Logothete and Prothonotary of the kingdom of Sicily. This reputable man, who had frequented the Dominican convent at Naples in his younger years as a student, made use of the reliable information of Dominicans who had been personally acquainted with Thomas. Chief among these was John of Cajatia, a preaching friar of great renown who was associated with Thomas (*multum familiaris*) and was his student at Paris and Naples. Moreover, Bartholomew of Capua, as a young student, personally saw and studied Thomas in Naples and was so impressed that the memory remained with him even in his old age.

Bartholomew of Capua began his description of the spiritual life and character of the saint in this manner:

> It was the common opinion of those who lived with Brother Thomas, especially some of the Friars Preachers most worthy of credence and respect, that the Holy Spirit was with him; for they always saw him with a serene countenance, meek, and humble. Never did he interfere with temporal affairs, but applied himself constantly to studies, lecturing, writing, and praying for the enlightenment of the faithful. I have heard from John of Cajatia that Brother Thomas was always

> the first to arise for prayers during the night, and as soon as he heard the others approaching, he withdrew and returned to his cell.

Bartholomew next recorded his personal impressions of the personality of St. Thomas, whom he observed whenever the opportunity presented itself:

> Brother Thomas always shunned petty matters, constantly searching after the sublime. He was a virgin, pure and chaste. No one could be found who had heard one vain word come from his lips. Even during disputations, in which men at times are apt to exceed the rule of moderation, he was always meek and humble, never using boastful or bragging language. He was so abstracted from temporal affairs that while he ate at table, his eyes were turned toward heaven. Dishes could be placed before him and removed without his taking notice. When the brethren brought him to the garden for recreation, he would suddenly go off alone, wholly abstracted from his surroundings, and return to his cell.

Some Dominicans, principally Nicholas Fricino, who attended the lectures of Brother Thomas and daily heard Mass at the convent of the Friars Preachers, revealed the following to Bartholomew:

> Brother Thomas celebrated his Mass every day in the early morning in the Chapel of St. Nicholas. When he had finished, another priest was ready immediately to celebrate another Mass. After hearing this Mass, he put aside the vestments and at once ascended the lecturing chair. His lectures being finished, he immediately began to write and dictate to numerous secretaries. After eating, he returned to his cell where he engaged in divine contemplation until time to rest. After this he would again assume his writing, and thus his whole life was ordered to God.[20]

The same witness heard many people express the common opinion that there was hardly a moment of time that he let pass uselessly. Bartholomew, who saw Brother Thomas for many years at Naples, and had spoken with many Dominicans, could recall but two occasions when he had seen him outside the cloister: once near the time of vespers; a second time in Capua at the royal court, where he went because of some difficulty concerning his nephew.

The canonization bull,[21] written by Pope John XXII on July 18, 1323, offers a summary of all the characteristics that we have found in the testimonies of his canonization. They comprise a uniform portrait of his soul and character. A few extracts indicate the principal thoughts of this ancient document. (The original, preserved in the archives of Toulouse, was publicized in photostatic reproductions on the occasion of St. Thomas's centenary.) After the pope had broadly outlined the life and the development of the saint to the heights of his scientific career as a professor of theology and creator of monumental philosophical and theological works, he described his saintly interior life:

> He accomplished all this as a skillful man, withdrawn from all earthly ambition and intent upon the attainment of heavenly goods. In applying himself to study, he put aside the temporal and strove after God so as to attain the eternal. He began with the divine in order to be fortified in his studies, when, each day before ascending the lecturing chair, he celebrated Mass and attended another, or, if he did not celebrate, attended two Masses. In these Masses as well as in his assiduous prayers, he revealed, in the shedding of tears, his sweetness of mind and his devotion to God, from whom nothing is hidden.
>
> He so shone in the splendour of chastity, carefully guarded with humility, and nourished by recollection, that many believed he remained incorrupt in the virginity of the flesh. The saint's confessor, who belonged to the same Order and

who had heard his confession for many years, also asserted publicly of him before all his friends: "I have heard the general confession of this holy man, of whom I testify that I have found him as pure as a boy of five years, for he never experienced the corruption of the flesh." This man of God, moreover, was content with the food of religious and the clothing of the common life. He was meek in conversation, pleasant in kindness, merciful in piety, subjected in humility, and adorned with many other virtues. He avoided the vanity of honors, and was cautious in his association with women. He never desired to be prominent. When engaged in a scholastic disputation, he never became so boastful as to use haughty words, as others frequently did, even if such words were used by his opponents. This servant of God was wholly intent upon divine works, sedulously applying himself to study in which he excelled, to preaching in which he was moving, to prayer in which he was devout, to Holy Writ which he understood so well. So it was that, aside from natural necessity or sleep, he never or rarely let any time pass in idleness.

CHAPTER 2

Characteristics of the Interior Life of St. Thomas

The testimonies that we have just examined from the acts of St. Thomas's canonization process are all similar and unified in praising him. The persevering routine of a scholar who devoted himself completely to God, to his vocation, and to his studies in the solitude of his cell does not resemble a torrent gushing down the high mountains but rather a peaceful and gently flowing brook that waters the fields and meadows. These everyday observations of the interior life of St. Thomas assume much livelier and brighter colors if we permit light from the works of the saint to fall upon them—if, from the depths of his own soul, we draw what he has written about the aims, laws, and ways of Christian virtue and perfection. These writings will form a sort of commentary on the testimonies of his canonization process.

In these testimonies, three basic features clearly stand out above the rest. Thomas is celebrated as a contemplative, as a thinker living totally in the world of the supersensory, the supernatural, and the divine. Furthermore, his glowing love of God, which finds its chief expression in his life of prayer and in the dedication of his whole life, exterior and interior, to God, is brought into prominence. Last, all these accounts extol his harmonious, well-balanced character, undisturbed and untroubled by any inordinate passion, since his virginal purity, humility, silence, modesty, meekness, benevolence, and amiability continually appear as the basic tendencies of his whole being. I would like to express these three fundamental traits in the words *wisdom*, *charity*, and *peace*.

I. Wisdom

The whole intellectual life of St. Thomas bears the imprint of wisdom; it is completely dedicated to contemplation and to the ordering of truth. In the paintings that depict the triumph of St. Thomas, art has expressed the root of this purest and noblest intellectuality, elevated to the heights of natural and supernatural contemplation of truth. We have such portrayals of the triumph of St. Thomas by Taddeo Gaddi in the Spanish chapel of S. Maria Novella at Florence; by Francesco Traini in the Church of St. Catherine at Pisa; by Filippo Lippi in S. Maria sopra Minerva; and by Benozzo Gozzoli in a tempera painting at the Louvre at Paris.

P.L. Ferretti, O.P., in his work that we have already mentioned, has reproduced and described two portrayals of the triumph of St. Thomas, which until now have remained generally unknown. One comes from the brush of Antonello da Messina,[22] and at present is found in the National Museum at Palermo. At the top of this painting, God the Father appears with two angels at His right, holding in their hands a book with the inscription: "*Bene scripsisti de me Thoma!*" (You have written well of me, Thomas!) At His left, two angels likewise hold a book with the words: "*Sensum tuum, Domine, quis scire poterit, nisi tu dederis sapientiam?*" (Oh Lord, who could know what you mean unless you gave wisdom?) Here, wisdom is pointed out as an essential feature of St. Thomas. In the middle of the portrait, the saint is seated upon a throne surrounded by angels. A pope is at his right, a king at his left. Farther to the rear, at his left, are clerics and religious; and at his right, lay people listen to his words. Averroes lies at his feet defeated and vanquished.

The second painting comes from the school of Antonello da Messina and is now preserved in the Museum of Palazzo Bellomo at Siracusa.[23] Here, Thomas is pictured upon the lecturer's chair. St. Peter stands to his right, while St. Paul is at his left. A crowd of listeners, both religious and lay, give ear to his teaching. Again, Averroes, whose intellectual defeat forms the fundamental idea in all these representations of the triumph of St. Thomas, is pictured at the bottom of the painting.

In the paintings of Traini and Gozzoli, the book that St. Thomas has opened before him bears, as the motto of his intellectual life's work, the words: "*Veritatem meditabitur guttur meum, et labia mea detestabuntur impium*" (My mouth shall meditate truth: and my lips shall hate wickedness) (Prov. 8:7). These are the exact words that Thomas placed at the beginning of his *Summa contra Gentiles* with which he explains the function of the wise man.

The greatest and most impressive of all these paintings is the triumph of St. Thomas (by Andrea di Bonaiuto, not Taddeo Gaddi) in the Cappellone degli Spagnoli at Florence. Here, St. Thomas is seated upon the lecturer's chair, holding an open book in which are the words: "*Optavi et datus est mihi sensus. Invocavi et venit in me spiritus sapientiae*" (Therefore I wished, and understanding was given me: and called upon God, and the spirit of wisdom came upon me) (Wisd. 7:7). P.J. Berthier, O.P., who explains in his weighty monograph the ideas of these portraits, pertinently remarks: "The whole life of the Doctor of Aquino is expressed in these words. Even in childhood he desired a higher and more divine knowledge. Thus at Monte Cassino, he asked the astounded teacher, 'What is God?' He prayed for knowledge and attained it; he longed for and implored a deep insight and received it. He prayed and the spirit of wisdom descended upon him. He left all: his noble name, parents, earthly prospects and hopes, in order to follow wisdom. He preferred wisdom to all honors."[24]

We are able to distinguish a threefold wisdom in which Thomas found the meaning and the happiness of life: *metaphysics*, which has already been characterized as σοφία by Aristotle; *supernatural theology*; and the *gift of wisdom*, the wisdom of the supernatural gift of the Holy Ghost, which lays the foundation for quasi-experimental knowledge of God, the loving and blessed contemplation of God.

Thomas is the greatest metaphysician of scholasticism and, in general, of all Christian philosophy. He unified into a magnificent and original synthesis the inductive and anthropocentric metaphysics of Aristotle, to which he wrote an approving commentary, and the theocentric metaphysics of St. Augustine. His metaphysical bent sought to reproduce in the mind the whole order of the universe and its causes. Father Garrigou-Lagrange, the best authority and representative of

Thomistic metaphysics in our day, characterizes the philosophy of St. Thomas as the philosophy of *being* in contrast to the modern philosophy that he describes as a philosophy of *becoming*, of phenomenalism.[25] Fr. Olgiati, an outstanding Italian philosopher, has represented, in his book *L'anima de San Tommaso*,[26] the metaphysics of *being* as the soul of the whole Thomistic system. Thomas rules the realm of facts and ideas from the heights of the science of *being*. Therefore, if one wishes to weigh and appreciate Thomas in all his genius and importance, he must take his stand here.

In this work, I do not intend to enter into the basic and fundamental questions of Thomistic metaphysics, into the doctrine of *being*, the real and universal validity of first principles, into his doctrine of potentiality and actuality, essence and existence, into the metaphysical coloring of his theory of knowledge, his ethics, and his aesthetics by the concepts of the ontological true, good, and beautiful, into his metaphysics of causes, and his theological consideration of the universe. I only wish to call attention briefly to two points: first, the importance of St. Thomas's metaphysical method of procedure for forming and systematizing his scientific structure; and second, the influence of this metaphysical outlook on his understanding of nature and the supernatural. These are considerations in which the weight of wisdom exerts its peculiar force: limiting, ordering, and supervising all from the highest principles.

The scientific formation and the order, so admired and worthy of admiration, of the thought and of the works of St. Thomas are not merely an external arrangement and an exact assembling of material, not merely a function and result of logical classification. Rather, it is an internal evolution in which lofty metaphysical and theological thoughts and views, in their conclusions, applications, and relations, pervade and govern, as dominating principles, the whole intellectual structure, giving it a perfectly unified style. The external arrangement is only the appearance, the garment of this inner order, which grows by organically developing and forming a central idea. In the *Summa Theologica*, the unsurpassable monument of Thomistic architectonics, we see this metaphysical approach in its inner union with and mutual penetration by the sublime thoughts of supernatural revelation.

This systematic development and organic unfolding of Thomistic metaphysics is manifested in its purest form in the first three books of the *Summa contra Gentiles.* The perspectives of the philosophico-theological structure of

St. Thomas most clearly and effectively unveil themselves when, throughout the whole system, we observe these fundamental thoughts of metaphysics in their consequences and applications, as Thomists of ancient and recent times have done with great profit.

The metaphysics of St. Thomas is not merely an arrangement of ideas but stands in living relationship with reality. It is a basic conviction of his philosophy that the human mind, chiefly by abstraction, then also by intuition and inference, is able to discover *being* and the laws and relations of *being* in experienced reality. It can perceive an agreement between the laws of *being* and the structure of the mind, the *ratio* in both a subjective and objective sense, which has its ultimate foundation in God, the First Cause of *being* and thought.[27]

The supreme laws of *being* in their transcendent validity, surpassing the limits of empiricism, are similar to unshakable pillars upon which our knowledge of causes lays the bridge to a knowledge of God. The metaphysical doctrine on the analogy of *being* teaches that *being* is not said about God and about creatures in a univocal or identical sense, nor in an equivocal or entirely different and improper sense, but rather in a similar sense relating the finite effect to the infinite cause. This doctrine points out, for our knowledge of God and the world, the true middle way between Monism on one side and Agnosticism and pure symbolism on the other. The metaphysical doctrine of potency and act, of the real distinction between essence and existence in creatures, helps to bring out clearly and precisely, in the Thomistic system, the basic distinction between God and the world, the transcendence of God over the world. On the other hand, careful reflection upon the universal divine causality, embracing the innermost *being* and activity of creatures, gives a profound understanding of the immanence of God in the world. These are but a few indications of the influence of St. Thomas's metaphysical approach on the formation and systematization of his philosophical and theological thought.

Here, likewise, I can express myself only briefly on the second point—the influence of this metaphysical viewpoint on the understanding of nature and the supernatural by St. Thomas. If one reads the main theological works of Thomas, above all his *Summa Theologica*, the philosophical, especially the metaphysical, expositions seem to take up so much space in totally theological contexts that the supernatural, the purely theological part, withdraws into the background. This seems so especially in comparison to the writings of other great scholastics, such as, perhaps, St.

Bonaventure. The intellectual structure of St. Thomas has given the impression of rationalism to many earnest students. And yet, this is far from the truth.

None of the great Catholic theologians of the Middle Ages has so precisely and clearly drawn the distinction between the natural and supernatural, between faith and reason, between philosophy and theology. And since he so accurately distinguished, he also very clearly defined the natural and supernatural, faith and reason, philosophy and theology, and showed their harmony as well.[28] Philosophical and theological tendencies, on the other hand, which at first glance may seem to bear much more the stamp of the supernatural, such as Jansenism, traditionalism, and ontologism, have blotted out the distinction between the natural and the supernatural. In fact, they so obscured the supernatural that they eventually reduced it to nothing.

The distinction as well as the harmony between the natural and the supernatural, faith and reason, philosophy and theology rest, according to St. Thomas, upon the rock foundation of metaphysical convictions. God, the Absolute Being, is the First Principle and First Cause of all finite natural *being*, which by reason of the divine act of creation is in the natural order a participation in the divine *being*. God, whose infinite plenitude of *being* and intelligence towers above all natural knowledge in the mysterious fecundity of the intimate life of the Trinity, is also the cause of the supernatural. Through a divine act of love and grace, the created soul is elevated to a participation in this mysterious life of God; it is raised to a sublime form and degree of union with God far exceeding all our natural expectations and abilities. The two rays of natural and supernatural truth, which are used in reason and faith, philosophy and theology, also flow from the bosom of God, the Absolute Eternal Truth. These are precisely the metaphysical convictions that bring Thomas to affirm the harmony between the natural and the supernatural orders of truth.

The great truths of metaphysics, the supreme laws of *being*, which simultaneously are laws of thought, are anchored— as St. Thomas teaches in conjunction with St. Augustine—in the intellect and nature of God, having absolute validity in the domain of the natural as well as in the supernatural order. Even the supernatural truths revealed by God fit within the framework of the highest metaphysical truths, although in themselves they are enthroned far above the pinnacles of metaphysics. Following the teaching of St. Thomas, the contingent physical order can be interrupted through the omnipotence of God for a proof of a divine revelation and mission. Yet, between the unshakable principles of metaphysics and the truths of supernatural revelation, no actual opposition can exist. The scientific doctrine of St. Thomas Aquinas, as it is developed principally in his profound work *In Boethium de Trinitate*, shows the mutual dependence and unity of the various branches of human knowledge by reason of their metaphysical orientation, and also manifests the harmony between the natural and supernatural knowledge of truth.[29]

One will never thoroughly understand the philosophy or the theology of the Angelic Doctor, nor be able to penetrate to the depths of his supernatural consideration of God and the universe, unless he has devoted himself through ceaseless study to the metaphysical concepts in his works. The oldest scholars of St. Thomas, whose works are constantly becoming better known through manuscript research, have plunged themselves directly into these metaphysical problems in the spirit of their much-beloved teacher. At the close of the Middle Ages, the Dominicans Paulus Soncinas and Dominicus of Flanders exposed the Aristotelian-Thomistic metaphysics in enormous works. In our day, since an ardent desire for metaphysics captivates the minds of many, the metaphysics of St. Thomas has not lost its sublime worth, so proved in the intellectual warfare of centuries. Thus Pope Pius XI writes in his encyclical in honor of St. Thomas (June 29, 1923): "And although his metaphysical teachings have aroused the bitterness of hostile critics, yet they still retain their force and splendour like pure gold that no acid can dissolve or tarnish."

Catholic philosophers, such as R. Garrigou-Lagrange, O.P., J. Maréchal, S.J., C. Beaumker, J. Geyser, and others, have demonstrated in numerous ways, by the contrast between St. Thomas's metaphysics and the modern current of thought, that Thomistic metaphysics has not lost its significance in the current intellectual strife.[30] Even thinkers outside Catholic and scholastic circles, who from prejudice oppose metaphysics, come unconsciously, and even consciously, to convictions in epistemology and metaphysics that are not far from the fundamental concepts of Thomistic metaphysics. An eminent natural philosopher of our time, who combines a very thorough scientific specialization with philosophical acumen, writes as follows:

> My conviction is rooted in the intellectual school of Aristotle and his followers of the Middle Ages, Albert the Great and Thomas

> Aquinas. While Albert already claimed experience to be the sole source of truth in scientific research, credit goes to St. Thomas for having established the principle of causality (no effect is without its cause) as the basis of philosophy and therefore also of natural science. Thomas realized, furthermore, that the relation of cause and effect did not suffice as an explanation of natural phenomena, but that for living things there must be an intellectual being as director and governor of nature, because of the undeniable finality and teleology manifested in them: Thus by a twofold consideration, namely, by the principles of causality and finality, Thomas concluded the existence of God from created nature.[31]

The second and loftier form of wisdom is theology, *sacra doctrina* (the sacred science), as St. Thomas loves to call it.[32] While metaphysics, the queen of all natural knowledge, is purely human, natural wisdom and science, theology is the human-divine wisdom and science. Theology is divine in its principles, the mysteries of faith revealed by God, and in its supernatural divine faith with which we assent with absolute certitude to these truths. It is human in drawing conclusions, chiefly with the help of philosophy, from the truths of faith; it is human in uncovering and unfolding the depths and relations of truths hidden in revealed doctrines. Metaphysics, in its ultimate and loftiest consideration, is also a science of things divine. But in so far as all philosophy is ordained to a knowledge of God through creatures, metaphysics is only a knowledge of God acquired by human reason climbing, from below, a ladder of causes. Metaphysics is a knowledge of divine things as we see them (*secundum nostrum modum*), a knowledge fitted to our natural intellectual life and never exceeding it.

Theology, on the other hand, is a knowledge of divine things as they are in themselves (*secundum modum ipsorum divinorum*), going beyond the natural capacity of our mind, oriented to God's knowledge of Himself, suited to the supernatural character of the mysteries of faith. It is a knowledge of the divine mysteries seen from the viewpoint of divine wisdom itself. This God-formed, if we wish to call it such, knowledge of divine things will be possible and complete only in Heaven, in the eternal unveiled vision of God. The present supernatural theology is merely a participation of the celestial theology, similar to the knowledge of God Himself in so far as through infused faith it adheres to God, the First Truth, on account of Himself.[33]

Thomas expresses his lofty conception of the nature of theology in the sentence: "*Sacra doctrina est velut quaedam impressio divinae scientiae, quae est una et simplex omnium.*"[34] Sacred science, in a certain sense, is an impression, a stamping of divine knowledge upon our mind, and thus it participates in the properties of God's knowledge, in His unity and simplicity. With good reason, one points to Raphael's *Disputa* as the representation of theological science, which is subordinated to the science of God and the Blessed.

For Thomas, theology is not merely science and the highest of all the sciences, but rather wisdom—*sapientia divina.* The saintly Doctor teaches:

> Theology is wisdom in so far as it considers the highest causes.... It is said to be wisdom more so than metaphysics for it considers the highest causes according to the mode of the causes themselves, since it is accepted immediately from God through revelation. Metaphysics, on the other hand, considers the highest causes from viewpoints taken from the realm of creatures. Hence this doctrine (theology) is said to be more divine than metaphysics, for it is divine in respect to the subject and the approach, whereas metaphysics is divine only in respect to the subject.[35]

Since St. Thomas elevates the science of theology to wisdom, he thereby gives it an eminent ethical significance, stressing the intimate, mutual relation between theology and life. For this reason, Thomas frequently emphasizes the importance of supernatural, ethical purity and sanctity for a theological knowledge. Life precedes doctrine and science; life leads to a knowledge of truth. In other sciences, it suffices that man be perfect intellectually. The divine science, on the contrary, demands perfection of intellect and affection.[36] Especially in chastity and humility, Thomas sees helpful dispositions for a deep and fruitful understanding of theology. The purpose of a chaste, virginal life consists in this—that man, unhampered by sensual desire, can devote himself to the contemplation of divine things (*liberius divinae contemplationi vacat*).[37] In pride, Thomas sees an obstacle to true science and wisdom, fruitful for thought and life, in so far as the proud person takes delight in his own supposed greatness and glory, and consequently loses the reverence and loving understanding for the excellence of truth. Humility, on the other hand, makes man broad and receptive toward God: "Humility makes man capable of God."[38]

With extraordinary warmth, St. Thomas stresses the influence of the supernatural virtue of charity and the gifts of the Holy Ghost, especially the gifts of understanding and wisdom, for a fruitful acquisition of theology. Thus we are led to the third consideration of wisdom, the gift of the Holy Ghost. In his commentary on the Gospel according to St. John, St. Thomas writes: "For just as a lamp is not able to illuminate unless a fire is enkindled, so also a spiritual lamp [by this Thomas refers to the priest, the theologian as student and preacher of supernatural truth] does not illuminate [i.e., receive and then give to others a profound understanding of the truths of faith] unless he first burn and be inflamed with the fire of charity. Hence ardor precedes illumination, for a knowledge of truth is bestowed by the ardor of charity."[39]

The gift of understanding confers a supernatural acuteness, a deep and clear insight into the mysteries of faith. The gift of wisdom, which has as a foundation the affective union of the soul with God, by sharing in the intimacy of the divine nature, gives an affective knowledge of divine things that depends upon this inner union of life and love with God and the divine.[40] Wisdom permits us to discover and taste these divine mysteries, especially the most secret workings of God in the soul filled with grace, and gives a loving and blissful quasi-experimental knowledge of God, a contemplation of divine realities, founded upon love and flowing again into love. To behold the unfathomable depths of God, to direct our vision toward God, to rejoice in the contemplation of the divine and thereby to be inflamed to a new love—to do all this out of love under an impulse of the Holy Ghost, who is personal divine Love, is the effect of the gift of wisdom, which here, before all else, is the principle of mystical contemplation and union with God. If Thomas is characterized with such insistence in the testimonies of the canonization process as a contemplative, then certainly we have full right to think about the gift of wisdom and mystical contemplation.

In the Middle Ages and at present, opinions have been advanced that desired to exclude St. Thomas from the history of mysticism because of his Aristotelian intellectualism. The Carthusian Vincent of Aggsbach, defender of an anti-intellectual mystical movement, wrote at the close of the Middle Ages that St. Thomas had not once even faintly mentioned mystical theology in his whole *Summa* as well as in his other works (*nec tenuem mentionem de mystica theologica facit*).[41] Recently, the Benedictine Abbot Butler,[42] highly respected in patrology and the history of monasticism, expressed a similar view.

The history of mystical theology is the best refutation of this assertion. The German mystics of the Order of Preachers, in so far as they do not fall under the influence of Neoplatonism, the Benedictine mystics, John of Castel, Bernard of Waging, and others, especially the Spanish mystics of the sixteenth and seventeenth centuries, and St. Francis de Sales in his *Theotimus*—all came under the inspiration of St. Thomas. From the mystical literature of the present day, I need only refer to the works in the *La Vie Spirituelle* by Fr. Garrigou-Lagrange, from whose pen have come the comprehensive works *Perfection chrétienne et Contemplation selon S. Thomas d'Aquin et S. Jean de la Croix* and *Traité de théologie ascétique et mystique, Les trois âges de la vie intérieure prélude de celle du ciel.*[43]

Father Gardeil, O.P.,[44] one of the most versatile and profound Thomists of our day, in a beautiful book on the gifts of the Holy Ghost in the Dominican saints, designates as the characteristic intellectual gift of St. Thomas not the gift of understanding, as one would expect, but rather the gift of wisdom. He bases this choice upon the attraction of the saint toward a contemplation of divine truths, toward a loving penetration into the depths of the mysteries of God. Not only in doctrine but also in life, Thomas was a contemplative. He was, as Lavaud writes in his description of St. Thomas's sanctity,[45] a contemplative soul similar to a St. John of the Cross. His life is rich in experiences that belong to the highest form of mysticism.

William of Tocco, relying upon the testimony of Reginald of Piperno, who in turn was allowed to see all the secrets of this beautiful and holy soul entirely dedicated to God, reports many occurrences of mystical conversation with a higher world. Mystical contemplation, especially toward the end of his life in Naples, was so intense and lasting that he suspended his literary activity (*suspendit organa scriptionis*). To the request of Reginald that he should write further and bring his works to their completion, Thomas answered: "Reginald, I cannot; for all that I have written appears as straw compared to what I have seen. I hope that God will soon prepare an end to my life and teaching."[46]

We can thus consider wisdom, in the threefold sense of metaphysics, of theology, and of mystical contemplation, as the character of St. Thomas's intellectual life. In him, we meet these three kinds of wisdom in all their individuality and difference, but always in full harmony. We agree with Lavaud's statement that whoever would fully understand the mutual harmony of these three forms of wisdom in the soul of St. Thomas would penetrate and understand the innermost depths of his whole interior life.[47] Thomas began his literary activity in a most promising way with the work *De Ente et Essentia*, an ingenious ground plan of metaphysics. At the height of his scientific labors, he wrote his *Summa Theologica* in which he combines metaphysics, speculative theology, and mystical intuition. On his death-bed in the cloister cell at Fossanova, he expounded to the monks the *Canticle of Canticles*, the song of loving mystical contemplation.

Fr. Lacordaire, O.P.,[48] notes as one of the first qualities of a theologian the ability to discriminate in applying the human, natural element to the religious sphere and observes that St. Thomas had this qualification to a very eminent degree. Thomas created a philosophy in whose veins flowed the blood of Aristotle, purified, however, by his own blood and the blood of earlier Christian thinkers. With this ability for differentiating when using the human or finite element, St. Thomas united a life deeply immersed in the divine element. He possessed a penetrating insight, symbolized by the eagle of St. John, into the contemplation of divine mysteries, a keenness of vision that is so difficult to define, yet recognizable if one, after his own reflection on some truth of Christianity, questions someone else whose ear has perceived the voice of the Infinite and has plunged more deeply into this abyss of God's mysteries. In this respect, a great theologian is similar to a great artist. The one, like the other, beholds what the ordinary eye never sees; both hear what the ear of the crowd cannot possibly detect. Such is the power of a discoverer in the region of the infinite, the intellectual apprehension of an infinite horizon, which constitutes and blesses, according to Lacordaire, a great theologian.

The lectures of St. Thomas permit us to recognize such a genius, who, with the greatest certainty of possessing divine truths, boldly soars to the heights, where an endless panorama of truth looms before the amazed and enraptured intellect. If one has studied a problem from the works of famous men, so Lacordaire continues, and then returns to Thomas, he feels that in him and with him with one flight he has traversed a broader expanse of truth. The great French orator also extols this solidity of order in which Thomas, subordinating always the human to the divine, joins the natural with the supernatural. Thus a wonderful unity arises, which never contradicts itself in this tremendous scientific work. In St. Thomas's style, Lacordaire sees the true appearance of the inner nature of his science and wisdom. This is a style that permits the truth to be seen in all its profundity, as a man sees the fish on the bottom of a placid sea, or sees the stars shine through a clear sky. It is a style peaceful and transparent, at once without fancy and emotion, delighting and fascinating the intellect.

II. Charity

The second feature in our portrait of the soul and character of St. Thomas, which unfolds itself from the acts of the canonization process, is charity—a most fervent, glowing love of God and neighbor.

Charity molded his whole life, directed all his works toward a divine service of God, finding its most touching expression in his life of prayer. We have already noticed this particular aspect in our discussion of the gift of wisdom, the mystical characteristic of his intellectual life.

The testimonies of the canonization process now receive additional light and confirmation from the writings of the saint. His questions on charity, on the Christian ideal of perfection, on the religious state in the *Secunda Secundae*, the *quaestio disputata de charitate*, the profoundly intimate passages in his commentaries on Sacred Scripture, especially on St. John's Gospel and the Pauline letters, all offer us a theology of charity. One realizes their beauty and sublimity the better, the more often and more meditatively he reads these texts.[49] Beams of light and love simultaneously emanate from these passages and give the impression that only a theologian in whose heart the divine fire of love brilliantly glows can so write about this divine charity.

Aristotelian intellectualism has soared to its heights in St. Thomas's treatment of divine charity. Through Thomas, this philosophy finds an independent, evident, and purposeful realization. More than any other system, it offers means of explaining the ultimate and more intricate questions of philosophy, and the origin and development of the supernatural order, which rests on the inner trinitarian life of God.

For this life on earth, St. Thomas proposes the principle that the love of God is better and more valuable than the knowledge of God, and he teaches us the comforting doctrine that we can love God more than we can know Him.[50] The mystics, for example, Blessed John Castel, have gratefully taken over this beautiful and encouraging thought.

While Aristotle views the θεωρία τῆς ἀληθείας (contemplation of truth) as the end and completion of this earthly sojourn, St. Thomas considers charity, the supernatural virtue of love of God and neighbor, as the end and ideal of the Christian life. This love permits us to strive after God, in so far as it unites the affections of man to

God, so that man himself no longer lives but rather God.[51] Since the Christian supernatural life consists in charity, in love, the perfection of this life consists, according to St. Thomas, in the perfection of charity, in the love of God and neighbor.

There is a perfection of love of God that belongs to God alone since He alone can love with an infinite love, as He, the absolutely highest Good, deserves to be loved.[52] The Holy Ghost, the personal divine Love through whom the love of God is infused into our hearts, proceeds from the love of the Father and the Son in the intimate life of the Trinity. A second degree in the perfection of the love of God is in the realm of the finite and proper to the Blessed in Heaven. Their total knowledge and love are uninterruptedly ordered in one continuous act toward God, the unveiled divine Love, whom they contemplate face to face. Their whole activity and life are an eternal, ineffably brilliant, glowing, and blessed ecstasy of love in this vision, enjoyment, and embrace of the infinite triune God.

This *semper actu ferri in Deum*, this perfection of love, in which the affection, in so far as it is able, is always actually directed toward God, is not possible here below because of the union of body and soul, because of the poverty of our earthly existence. Yet, wherever Thomas speaks of the perfection of charity, this unbroken loving dedication of the heart and the whole man to God, these continuously intimate acts renewing our dependence upon God hover before him as the ideal toward which we are to strive even during this life.

Thomas sought to realize this ideal in himself, to the degree possible on this earth, by a life totally removed from the things of this world, according to the testimonies of the canonization process. Vincent Contenson, O.P.,[53] writes in his *Theologia mentis et cordis* that Thomas is the Angelic Doctor not only because of his angelic purity and chastity and because of his keen intellect, which pierced the depths of truth, but also because he was living spiritually with the angels in Heaven, although still lingering with his body upon the earth.

For this life on earth, St. Thomas distinguishes between a perfection of love that is obligatory and necessary for all and a perfection of love that surpasses the ordinary degree, constituting the object of the evangelical counsels.

The first degree of love consists in ordering all to God as to one's final end, in subjecting one's whole life to the service of God, and in avoiding mortal sin, which turns us away from God as from our final supernatural end. The second and more ennobled form of the perfection of love that we can attain upon this earth consists in the greatest possible striving after the heavenly perfection of charity, in practicing the most fervent, actual, and constant loving conversation and devotion of the soul with God. This perfection is manifest in the liveliness, the activity, the fiery zeal of love pressing forward into action, in the *fervor charitatis*. Such a fervor of charity, which St. Thomas stresses so much in his writings, permeated his whole being and life, permitting him to labor simply and solely for the glory of God in a holy, humble forgetfulness of self until the very consumption of all his bodily strength. It let him see and attain the ideal of his order (*contemplata aliis tradere*) in the union of the contemplative and active life.

The life of St. Thomas was an undisturbed clinging to God, manifesting itself in fervent deeds, "an adhering to God through charity"—as if he preferred the use of the expression "adhere" to "inhere." The result and expression of this *fervor charitatis*, of this undivided and unhampered adherence to God through charity, was a deep and heartfelt dedication through prayer and study to an unbroken service of his mind and heart to God.

The soul will be the more inflamed by the fire of this love, the actuality and vitality of this love will proportionately increase, according as the soul detaches itself from all earthly relations, even from those in themselves tolerable and reconcilable with the state of grace. Now come into play the evangelical counsels, whose observance releases the soul of man from attachment to material things, permitting the soul to give itself up to God in a wholly free and unhindered manner. They fill us with a holy longing to belong to God completely, to sacrifice to God everything that we are and have, to fulfill in all things the most holy will of God as well as letting its fulfillment take place in us: "All the counsels, by which we are called to perfection, tend to withdraw the heart of man from the love of temporal affairs, so that the mind can more freely turn to God in contemplating, loving, and fulfilling His will."[54] Voluntary poverty severs us from attachment to earthly goods. Perpetual chastity and virginity enable us to serve God with a clean heart and pure love, and being thus freed, to cling and devote ourselves totally to God. In obedience, the Christian, forsaking self, offers his will to God in sacrifice.

These evangelical counsels form the essence of the religious state. In his *Summa Theologica*,[55] as well as in his three other works written in defense of the religious ideal, especially in the excellent work *De Perfectione Vitae*

Spiritualis, Thomas, in a very profound and yet clear exposition, has most beautifully and strikingly expressed whatever has been scientifically written on the nature of the religious state. Only he who has grasped this state in all its depth and extension, who has taken upon himself all its consequences, who has embraced it with the sum-total love of his own heart, can so write about the religious state.

The acts of the canonization process depict Thomas as a holy, perfect religious. They tell us about his ardent desire to live until the end of his life in the quiet of the cloister simply and solely for his God, sacred science, and the religious calling. With tears, he requested Pope Clement IV to cancel his nomination as archbishop of Naples. Another earnest request of his prayer was to remain a simple religious to the very end of his life. His prayer was heard—his wish fulfilled. The great theologians of his order rose to high ecclesiastical dignities: his teacher, Albert the Great, became bishop; his friend, Annibaldo Annibaldi, became cardinal; his colleague as a professor at the University of Paris, Peter of Tarentaise, became cardinal and later pope. Also, his friend in nobility, Adenulf of Anagni, the nephew of Gregory IX, a professor at Paris, of whom we know too little, was elected to the bishopric of Paris upon his entrance into the cloister of St. Victor.

Thomas, the greatest of them all, died a simple Friar Preacher at Fossanova.

Here I cannot discuss in greater detail how Thomas likewise explained the perfection of Christian love of neighbor, and how he clearly distinguished between the practice of virtue that is obligatory for all and that which is the object of the counsels. The heights to which St. Thomas elevated love of neighbor is manifested when he admonishes, under certain circumstances, that the contemplative life, which he considers to be intrinsically of greater value than the active life, be interrupted and even abandoned in order to devote ourselves to the service and salvation of our neighbor's soul.

In a passage from his work *De Perfectione Vitae Spiritualis*, which describes, with the living colors of his own interior life and heroic disposition, the abounding perfection of a holy, devoted love of neighbor, he enunciates the following beautiful principle: "And in so far as contemplation is superior to activity, so much the more would he appear to work for God, who, at the expense of his much-loved contemplation, labors for his neighbor's salvation because of God. Therefore, to labor for the salvation of our neighbor, even at the expense of contemplation, for the love of God and neighbor, appears to be a higher perfection of charity than if he would cling so dearly to the sweetness of contemplation as to be totally unwilling to sacrifice it even for the salvation of others."[56] These thoughts we likewise meet in the German mystics Eckhart and Tauler.[57]

In his life and writings, St. Thomas resolutely held the principle that he clearly understood and consequently lived—charity is the form of the virtues, giving perfection, activity, unity, worth, and direction to the whole supernatural Christian life of virtue. For the higher degrees of striving after perfection, purified of earthly affairs and devoted to God, St. Thomas has described, in a way only one living and seeking after perfection can, this elevation and glorification of the whole interior life through charity and the gifts of the Holy Ghost connected with charity. He has described noble souls who constantly seek through humility and penance to purge themselves from all stains and imperfections that oppose in any way the ideal of purity and sanctity seen in God: souls who joyfully and generously respond to the inspiration of the Holy Ghost even when this summons the most severe and painful resolution on the part of man to act and to suffer. Love of God and neighbor expresses itself in these heroic souls in the holiest and noblest dispositions, in ardent and fervent interior deeds, and in an exterior activity compatible with an ordinary way of life.

In one passage, St. Thomas has shown, with remarkable conciseness, clarity, and beauty, how the cardinal virtues are completely imbued with and enlivened by charity as their form in a purified soul living only for God.[58] In so far as the cardinal virtues order the natural and social life of man [acquired moral virtues], they are called "social" virtues. In so far as the cardinal virtues orient themselves to the ideal of divine sanctity, supernaturally known and loved, and are concerned with the higher ways of Christian perfection, lifted above everything natural and material [infused moral virtues], they become partly "perfecting" virtues and partly "perfect" virtues. The former [infused moral virtues imperated by charity] completely purify the soul and dispose it for the contemplative union with God, while the latter [infused moral virtues in their specific act] are virtues of life making possible imitation of and union with God here and in Heaven.

As perfecting virtues, prudence despises all earthly things for the contemplation of the things of God and directs the whole intellectual vision unswervingly to the divine. Temperance frees one, in so far as nature permits, of all corporeal comfort and pleasure. Fortitude gives the soul the courage and strength wholeheartedly to undertake the trials and sacrifices of this complete detachment from earthly and corporeal things and to apply itself without stint to supernatural and heavenly things. Justice makes the soul agree to this holy resolution to lead such a life. In such few short strokes, the saint has pictured the cardinal virtues in their Christian, supernatural elevation, in their proper place within the framework of Christian perfection.

These virtues receive an even more sublime meaning as perfect virtues, virtues completely detached from the world, which unite and make us similar to God. Prudence considers now only the divine; temperance recognizes no sensual desires; fortitude no longer feels the vehemence of the passions; justice, in imitation of the Divine Mind, is united in an everlasting bond with the spirit of God. The Blessed in Heaven and a few very perfect souls upon earth properly possess the cardinal virtues in their perfection. In such a description of the twofold aspect of the cardinal virtues, which are animated by charity, Thomas has sketched, without ever intending it, a portrait of his own pure and holy inner life in which charity is truly the form, the entelechy of the virtues.

In another place where he treats of the conjectural knowledge regarding our state of grace, he proposes as a criterion that anybody is in the state of grace and charity *in quantum percipit se delectari in Deo et contemnere res mundanos.*[59] Anybody can know with moral certitude sufficient for a Christian life of virtue and for seeking after perfection that he is in the state of sanctifying grace and love if he, according to the testimony of his conscience, finds his happiness in God and pays little attention to the things of this world. In these simple words, St. Thomas has revealed the basic state of his own inner life. In God alone, he found his joy, satisfaction, and the fulfillment of all his desires and quests. In comparison to this happiness of lovingly clinging to God, all that is temporal and perishable appeared to him empty and insufficient to completely satisfy the human person, who, according to knowledge and love, is made for the infinite.

For St. Thomas, spiritual joy (*gaudium spirituale*) is an effect of charity, which is prior to all the other effects that flow from this love.[60] The *fervor charitatis*, the lively devotion of love toward God, busying itself in the most frequent and fervent deeds, is the principal source of the most pure supernatural beatitude of soul. Devotion, the consecration of the heart and mind to God in the practices of piety, in which the *fervor charitatis* expresses itself most ardently, has spiritual happiness (*laetitia spiritualis*) as its special effect. This happiness issues from a devout meditation on and contemplation of the divine goodness, although thoughts on the suffering of Christ and on our own sins and sinfulness fill us simultaneously with a holy sorrow.[61] The tears that are shed in true prayer to God do not flow merely from grief but also from a certain tenderness of heart. Such is especially the case when one contemplates a religious subject in which joy is mingled with sorrow.[62] Here the saint can speak from his own experience since both the testimony of his canonization process and the bull of canonization tell us that he shed abundant tears during his prayers.

The fervor of charity and spiritual delight are intimately connected in the Most Holy Eucharist, in Holy Communion. Holy Communion, especially if received without the impediments of deliberate venial sin, distraction, and an inordinate earthly attachment, causes not only a strengthening and increase of habitual love but also an enkindling to ardent acts of love, to a *fervor charitatis*. This *excitatio caritatis ad actum*, this inflaming to divine acts of love, is the source of spiritual joy, of spiritual delight that overflows into the soul from such devout communions. St. Thomas speaks of an effect of Holy Communion that he calls a *quaedam actualis refectio spiritualis dulcedinis*, a refreshing of the soul with spiritual sweetness, consummating itself in holy and ardent acts of love.[63] The following words of St. Thomas, in which he describes this effect of the Holy Eucharist, are of stirring beauty and depth:

> The love of God is never idle, for wherever it is, it does great works. Consequently through this sacrament, as far as it lies in its power, it not only bestows the habit of grace and virtue, but also arouses us to act, according to 2 Cor. 5, 14: "The charity of Christ presseth us." Hence it is that the soul is spiritually nourished through the power of this sacrament, in so far as it is spiritually gladdened, and as it were inebriated with the sweetness of the divine Goodness, according to Cant. 5, 1: "Eat, O friends, and drink, and be inebriated, my dearly beloved."[64]

Only a soul can so write who has experienced in Holy Communion the actual fervor of devotion,[65] the fire of love perfecting itself in ardent acts of piety and devotion, who has tasted from his own experience the blessedness and ineffable happiness resulting from union with Jesus in Holy Communion. This state of mind and feeling is expressed in the hymn *Adoro te devote*, in which the saint implores and prays:

Panis vivus, vitam praestans homini,
Praesta meae menti de te vivere
Et te illi semper dulce sapere.

✠ ✠ ✠

O living Bread, to mortals life supplying!
Make Thou my soul henceforth on Thee to live;
Ever a taste of heavenly sweetness give.

The office of Corpus Christi, which St. Thomas wrote at the request of Pope Urban IV, breathes a very similar spirit, and thus his name has always been connected with the liturgy of the Eucharist.[66] John of Cologne, O.P., in his beautiful and profound poetry, says concerning this office: "This blessed and holy Doctor composed the office of Corpus Christi, which is recited and chanted more devoutly than any other in the church."[67] For Thomas, rays of Christ's love for us and our love for Him are focused in the Most Holy Eucharist. "The Eucharist is the sacrament which expresses Christ's love and causes our love."[68]

The doctrine of Thomas on the Eucharist, as he portrayed it in the Third Part of his *Summa Theologica*, near the close of his life, blends the three forms of wisdom into a harmonious union. In his expositions, both profound and clear, on transubstantiation, on the manner of

Christ's presence in the Eucharist, and on the Eucharistic accidents, St. Thomas shows himself the master metaphysician even within the domain of theology. By harmoniously uniting the writings and teachings of the Fathers on the Most Holy Eucharist, and developing profound reasons of fitness, the Master of Dogma comes to the fore. In the idea, which he derived from his own innermost experience, on the *fervor charitatis* of the Eucharist, on the supernatural refreshment flowing from this active and inner love, and on the joy of soul resting upon the Heart of Jesus in Holy Communion, the mystical element makes its appearance in this triad of wisdom.

The interior life of St. Thomas manifests an undeniable attraction to the Holy Eucharist, without which consideration we cannot understand the inner depths of his soul. It is especially here that the basic priestly character of his whole being expresses itself. In the testimonies of his canonization process, we have heard again and again the burning devotion with which the saint celebrated the Holy Sacrifice of the Mass in the early hours of the morning, after which he attended a second Mass in thanksgiving. We do not know when or where St. Thomas was ordained a priest. History, however, has preserved for us the fervor and devotion with which he celebrated this most sublime function of the priestly office and with which he made his thanksgiving after the Holy Sacrifice. The daily celebration of the Mass presented a strong incentive for striving after interior purity and perfection. He insisted upon the obligation of priests to strive after an eminent degree of moral purity and sanctity because of the celebration of the Eucharistic banquet in the words: "Since one is appointed to the most august ministry of serving Christ Himself in the sacrament of the altar through Holy Orders, a greater inward holiness is required than that which is needed for the religious state."[69]

Art has also strikingly portrayed St. Thomas's intimate connection with the theology, liturgy, and mysticism of the Holy Eucharist. The monument of the saint at Toulouse in St. Sernin, which was destroyed during the French Revolution, acclaimed him as the *Doctor Eucharisticus*. Over the tomb is enthroned a beautiful picture of the saint. He holds the Holy Eucharist in one hand; in the other, a flaming sword. Underneath, there is the verse:

Ex Evangelii solio cherubinus Aquinas
Vitalem ignito protegit ense cibum.

✠ ✠ ✠

From the throne of the Gospel, Thomas, the Cherub,
Protects the living bread with a fiery sword.

The dominant theme of this painting is Thomas, the Cherubim of the Eucharistic mystery.

In S. Maria Novella at Florence, Orcagna's painting represents St. Thomas at the altar celebrating Mass in ecstasy.[70] In a painting by P.P. Rubens, which now is in the del Prado Museum at Madrid, St. Thomas extols the Holy Eucharist with a forceful gesture in the midst of the Fathers of the Church.[71] A procession moves before the artist. Gregory the Great, Augustine, and Ambrose proceed in the front, while Jerome and Bonaventure follow. St. Thomas, his countenance glowing, is placed in the middle of the painting as the principal figure. He holds a book in his right hand, and his left hand is raised enthusiastically proclaiming the praise of the Eucharist. At his left, a nun holds with both her hands a monstrance containing the Blessed Sacrament. Without a doubt, this nun is Juliana of Liège, who stimulated the first move for the institution of the feast of Corpus Christi.

In poetry, Calderón, above all, has acclaimed St. Thomas as the theologian and troubadour of the Blessed Sacrament. In one of his most beautiful *Autos sacramentales*, "Holy Parnassus," he represents the Church as lofty Parnassus, the holy mountain of true poetry, where the faithful unite in songs of praise around the

Eucharistic Lord, the true divine Apollo. The Sibyls, types of heavenly poetry, summon the Doctors of the Church, Jerome, Ambrose, Augustine, Gregory, and Thomas Aquinas to a lyrical contest in praise of the Blessed Sacrament. In this poetic competition, Thomas recites his *Pange Lingua.* For this, he receives, as a reward of victory, the sun upon his breast, the radiant emblem of enlightened wisdom and ardent love of God.

I am concluding these thoughts on charity, the second basic trait in the portrait of St. Thomas's soul and character, with the striking words of the Dominican A. Touron, who has written the most beautiful biography of our saint up to the present time:

> His words, perfectly conformed to his actions, make known the purity of his soul and the extent of his charity. We reach this conclusion by reading his works, principally those in which he treats of matters concerning the inner life: the perfection of the spiritual life, the gifts of the Holy Ghost, the various degrees of the moral virtues with the different ways of practicing them, the excellence and the fruits of contemplation, the eminence of charity, and all that occurs most intimately in the holy communication of a saintly soul with

God, its Father, Friend, and Spouse. In these wonderful treatises, the saint appears to depict himself, and to paint with true-to-life strokes the very depths of his inner life.... His oldest biographer, William of Tocco, has remarked that he did not dare to preach what he himself had not first practiced. We should never doubt that he had also experienced in the delights of prayer and in the holy exercise of the Christian virtues all that he had taught us in his writings. His doctrine, always pure, modest, and characterized by all those traits that the Apostle James (3, 17) attributes to wisdom coming from above, is itself a sure proof that his heart participated as much as his intellect in all that came from his pen to lead us to a knowledge of God and self.

In his works of piety St. Thomas speaks of the great mystery of the love which God has shown for us, either by uniting Himself to our nature to free us from our sins and to clothe us with His justice, or by giving Himself entirely to us to be our food, our consolation, and the token of our salvation. Now we clearly understand that they are not only the result of a lofty and fruitful intellect shedding light for our instruction, but also the holy effusion of a soul perfectly united to God, permitting some

> sparks of love with which it is inflamed to shine forth. We feel that his every word is the overflow of his heart which, in turn, imparts light and unction to them. Every stroke of his pen, as well as every action of his life, proceeds from the principle that made him write or act, and from the goal which he proposed for himself in all things—I refer to that pure love of God which animated his heart and directed his hand, as well as the ardent desire which he always had to live only according to the spirit of Jesus Christ.[72]

III. PEACE

The third feature of the soul and character of St. Thomas is peace—quiet, balance, harmony of soul—which flows naturally from wisdom and charity.

This peace gleams before us pure and tender as a reflection of the eternal peace of Heaven, in which order and harmony of soul are brought about and strengthened by faith and reason, charity, and the gifts of the Holy Ghost. Fra Angelico da Fiesole, who because of his angelic purity and gentle, kind disposition was like Thomas, understood this peace so as to portray it in his pictures that he painted of the greatest theologian of his order.

Peace is a fruit, an effect of charity—love of God and neighbor. The brighter and more intense this charity becomes, the more profound and pure the peace.[73] In the marvelous system of speculative theology, the beatitude that praises the peacemakers corresponds to the gift of wisdom: "Blessed are the peacemakers for they shall be called the children of God."[74]

Peace, the motto of the Order of St. Benedict, reveals a plenitude of inner happiness and heavenly peace known to God alone. St. Thomas breathed deeply of this peace of St. Benedict during his years of childhood on the holy heights of Monte Cassino, where one feels much nearer to Heaven. Such contemporary Dominicans as Mandonnet, Petitot, and Gigon[75] maintain that St. Thomas was an oblate of the Benedictine Order and wore the habit of St. Benedict. Had his father not removed him from the cloister (not in 1235 nor 1236, but perhaps first in 1237) in fear of a threatening war, he eventually would have belonged to the Benedictine Order.

We can perceive a Benedictine trait in his life and writings, even though he belonged to the Dominican Order. Providence had determined that in Naples, Thomas would dedicate his whole life to the Order of St. Dominic and that he would remain steadfast in his vocation despite the objections and obstacles raised by his family. He keenly understood and was deeply enkindled by the noble ideal of this order—the Order of Truth, which soon would assume the leading role in the flowering of Scholasticism through his influence. Nevertheless, the Order of St. Benedict feels itself drawn in a spirit of appreciation toward the Angel of the Schools. (Such sentiments are again apparent at this time.) In Thomas, *veritas* and *pax*, the watchwords of the Dominicans and the Benedictines chime in harmony: "*Veritas et pax osculatae sunt*" (Truth and peace embrace).

The English Benedictine R. B. Vaughan, in his huge biography of St. Thomas, points out that the spirit and effects of St. Thomas can never be fully understood without the mystical spirit of the Patriarch of the occidental monks—a spirit of meekness, kindness, and quiet, which the boy Thomas acquired in the metropolis of Benedictinism.[76]

Pax est tranquillitas ordinis (peace is the tranquility resulting from order). This thought of St. Augustine is fully realized in the interior life of St. Thomas. An incomparable order and harmony prevail primarily in his thought and outlook. Just as obscurity, uncertainty, and confusion of ideas cause restlessness and disquietude to overflow into the whole life of the soul, so, too, a clear, profound, and ordered knowledge of natural and supernatural truth with its principles and relations, in its multiplicity and unity, diffuses a pure, intellectual peace into the soul seeking after truth. The Dominican B. Allo, in a panegyric honoring St. Thomas, has characterized the individuality of Thomas's soul in the words: "*La paix dans la vérité*."[77]

The function of the wise man, as St. Thomas points out, is to order—to gain an ordered knowledge of truth that is ruled and guided by the highest principles and views. He must first discover and establish the natural order in the realm of logical thought, of real being, and of moral acts. Then he must superimpose the supernatural order of the intimate life of God in His revelation, brought about through Jesus Christ and bestowed upon rational creatures, who are elevated by grace to a participation in this divine life.

Here I cannot pursue any further how, in the system of St. Thomas, order, symmetry, peace, and temper of truth and clarity are manifested in every single detail: in his formal exposition and in his ability to grasp and harmonize the most diverse opinions. Faith and reason, philosophy and theology, nature and grace, universalism and individualism, analysis and synthesis, Augustinian spiritualism and Aristotelian realism—these and other conceptual antipodes, which have been distorted even within Scholasticism into various extremes and contradictions, have found a peaceful and harmonious symmetry in the thought of St. Thomas.

This balance, moderation, and clarity of judgment, this sense of finality and order are evidenced in a very striking and beneficial manner in the social and political teaching of St. Thomas, which certainly breathes the spirit of peace.[78] The same agreement and harmony also make their appearance in his use of sources.[79] With clear vision, he has discerned the pith of truth under the bark of error and has indicated the historical growth of philosophical and theological questions, gazing far beyond the scientific range of ideas proper to his time. With grateful appreciation, he has utilized the results thought out in previous ages, readily recognizing the indirect service afforded by false opinions for the discovery of truth: "When considering truth, we are aided by others in a twofold manner: directly and indirectly. We are helped directly by those who have found the truth, for, as has been said, when one has discovered the truth, gathering it into a unit, he bequeathes to posterity a great knowledge of truth. We are helped indirectly in so far as those who have previously erred concerning truth thereby furnish to posterity a stimulus for philosophizing, so that the truth may stand out more clearly after diligent discussion."[80]

A high degree of scholarly and well-balanced impartiality and prudence, a peaceful blending of piety and a criticism that is reasonable, objective, and occasionally even historical, is shown in the manner in which St. Thomas individually utilized and evaluated Aristotle and his Greek commentators, Arabian-Jewish philosophy, Neoplatonic sources, Augustine and the Fathers of the Church, the works of the early Scholastics, and those either immediately preceding or contemporary.

The more one examines and learns to appreciate the delicate and sensitive manner in which the saint wove together the varicolored threads of earlier elements of thought into a unified and brilliant tapestry in each and every question, as in epistemology and psychology, metaphysics and theodicy, ethics and mysticism, and the basis of sacramental theology, the more he will recognize and appraise the masterful intellectual work that Thomas has accomplished in completing and harmoniously forming this vast structure of thought. Here I cannot examine the way in which he used Aristotle and Augustine, nor his synthesis of Aristotle and Augustine, in which Harnack sees the worldwide importance of St. Thomas.[81]

St. Thomas's use of sources is neither a compilation and mechanical collection of various opinions and trends of thought nor a weak eclecticism; rather, it is his own penetration, formation, and furthering of the results of investigations made at his time. Thomas assimilated and evaluated this vast amount of scientific tradition in the service of truth—that truth that he had always before him: "The study of philosophy is not to know what men have thought, but what the truth of things is in itself."[82] The independent organizing and speculative genius of St. Thomas, which directed all known truth into unison, was the entelechy, the form assimilating, fashioning, and certifying extraneous elements of thought.

The French scholar P. Duhem, otherwise so noted for his historical scholastic research, especially in the field of natural science, is far from the truth when he denies in large part St. Thomas's own proper importance in philosophical thought.[83] We now see more clearly in the light of laborious manuscript research that the heated strife about his doctrine, which had been enkindled even during the lifetime of the great scholastic and which burst into flame after his death, began with the acceptance of the Christian Aristotelianism of St. Thomas as an independent achievement of the widest innovation.[84] R. Seeberg writes:

> There is no question that Thomas was the most modern of the theologians of his time, for he

> sought, so far as that was possible, to apply the thoughts of Aristotle, which filled his theology.... Thomas had a special aptitude for this type of work. How easily he knows how to condense the most complicated trains of thought into neat and simple forms. He was always able to coin the precise expression, for he was keen and clear, equipped with a sure insight for essentials, and had a marvelous dialectical ability. Consequently he was the proper person to effect securely and tactfully the very difficult combination of the teachings of the Fathers and the Aristotelian philosophy, to translate Augustine into Aristotelianism, and to borrow from Aristotle whatever the teaching of the Fathers did not directly oppose.[85]

Things new and progressive do not stand out discordantly or shockingly in St. Thomas's works, and when such doctrines are advanced, never or seldom does he make mention of their newness. His novel course follows, in large part, the middle path, refraining from extremes. The peace of a soul who seeks not self but only the truth, and ultimately God, the Eternal Truth, is diffused throughout the intellectual labors of Thomas.

The authority of the Church, to which Thomas was devoted with a childlike love, did not present an obstacle nor a hindrance to his progressive scientific endeavors. Rather, he saw and loved in the Church, in its doctrinal authority, tradition, liturgy, and practices, a God-given assurance of a certain knowledge of truth. He pierced incomparably deep into the inner nature of the Church and united the dogmatic and mystical, the ethical and juridical elements into a harmonious concept of the Church.[86] The Church has, as he relates, the good of the faithful in mind in all her decisions and instructions.[87] He makes known his great esteem for the authority of the Church when he writes: "The practice of the Church, which should be observed always and in all instances, has the greatest authority." Even the doctrine of the Fathers receives its authority from the Church: "Therefore it is better to adhere to the practice of the Church rather than to the authority of an Augustine, a Jerome, or of any other doctor."[88]

He shows the highest esteem and reverence toward the primacy of the pope. This primacy he derived dogmatically from the Pauline idea of Christ, the Head of the Church, and from the nature and end of the Church. (Thomas was personally acquainted with the popes of his time, namely Urban IV, Clement IV, and Gregory X.)

St. Thomas is filled with the greatest piety toward the Fathers of the Church. Even where he believes another opinion must be held, he chooses a form and manner in which there is no hint of blame or reproach. Thus in one place, he writes: "Since this opinion was held by great doctors, namely Basil, Gregory Nazianzus, and certain others, it should not be rejected as erroneous."[89] Cardinal Cajetan likewise mentioned this reverent, conciliatory attitude of Aquinas toward the Fathers: "Since the author had the greatest veneration for them, he was endowed, in a certain manner, with the intellectual acumen of them all."[90]

The impressive portrait of Fr. Zurbarán, the apotheosis of St. Thomas, now preserved in the museum at Seville, is, in a certain sense, an artistic commentary on this idea.[91] St. Thomas is standing in the middle upper portion of this magnificent painting. He is enlightened by the Holy Ghost, who hovers over him in the form of a dove. In his left hand, he holds an opened book; the uplifted right hand holds a quill—he is prepared to write. The four great Doctors of the Western Church, Augustine, Gregory, Ambrose, and Jerome, sit at his left and right with their books before them. They are busily engaged in conversation.

Thus the peaceful spirit of order, harmony, and balance is diffused throughout the writings of St. Thomas. This sense for mediating and harmonizing, this rhythm, if

I dare say so, of truth and clarity appears in his weighty treatment of problems as well as in his use of sources. Joy and peace will overflow into the soul of him who has been impregnated and quickened, through years of study, by this harmony and proportion of the Thomistic structure. A joy and peace will come to him, similar to that reverential feeling that enraptures us when we behold the towering cathedrals with which the *Summa Theologica* of St. Thomas is frequently compared because of its architectonic form.[92]

This same balance, prudent and moderate method, peace, and clarity of the Thomistic system manifest themselves most effectively in his exposition of Christian morals, ascetics, and mysticism in the *Second Part*, an exposition extolled by his admiring contemporaries. Charity, according to the words of St. Bernard, *modus diligendi Deum est sine modo diligere* (knowing neither bounds nor limits), confers, as the form of the virtues, measure and agreement to all the moral virtues. It tends to behold lovingly in God the harmony and unison of the divine perfections and to build and model our interior and exterior life in accordance with them. The moral virtues, informed by charity, order and quiet the inner movements and passions of the soul so that the soul, undisturbed and undivided, can adhere to God in a life of a more ardent and increasing love. Even the desire for knowledge, which curiosity, a vice thwarting higher achievements, can pervert, must be ordered and moderated by the virtue of studiousness.[93]

The arrangement and mutual order of all the virtues as treated in Thomistic morals show a great deal of wisdom and everyday experience. The asceticism and mysticism of St. Thomas vividly show the way in which the life of grace assimilates the principles of the human life of the soul and gently elevates the whole sensitive and intellectual man to the supernatural, divine life.[94] Fr. Raymond Martin, O.P., remarks that he has never found the mystical doctrine more humanly and at the same time more divinely presented than in the teaching of St. Thomas on the spiritual life.[95]

St. Thomas was able to present such an effective teaching on the virtues—a doctrine replete with harmony and balance, ruled and sustained by the one important consideration of love, over which hovers an ardent and holy peace—because this same harmony, balance, and proportion of the virtues flowing from the gentle streams of divine love governed his own soul, because such a peace, springing from wisdom and charity, illumined all his thoughts, desires, feelings, and actions. The modest reports of the witnesses at the canonization process have let us glance into this pure and holy soul, freed from inordinate movements of sense, from attachment to earthly goods, and from the desire for honors and sensuality. His spotless, virginal purity is praised in all these testimonies. The expression *virgo* recurs again and again.

The acts of the canonization process and his first biography by William of Tocco record the mystical experience of young Thomas in the tower of S. Giovanni when he was girded by angels following the conquest of a most trying temptation. Thereafter he never experienced the movements of sensuality.[96] Since Fra Angelico da Fiesole, this scene has often been portrayed in art. Its memory lives on in a Church confraternity, the Angelic Warfare, which pays special honor to St. Thomas as patron and model of moral purity and innocence.[97] The title "Angelic Doctor," which was bestowed on St. Thomas at a somewhat later period because of his angelic purity (*qua in carne praeter carnem vixit*, "while living in the flesh, he was not of the flesh"), has surpassed his original scholastic name of honor, "Common Doctor."

Thomas had such an esteem for the virtues of chastity and virginity because he saw in them a very special fitness for an exclusive dedication and consecration to God, for a total unfolding and exercise of wisdom and charity. This dominating thought appears again and again in the beautiful questions and articles that he has dedicated to this angelic virtue.[98] The Pauline thought: "The virgin thinks about the things of the Lord, that she may be holy in body and in spirit" (1 Cor. 7:34) has found a most profound interpreter in Thomas, who wrote from his own innermost experience. Likewise, his devotion to St. Agnes, whose relic he always carried with him, can only be understood in terms of his love for chastity and virginity. Twice she is mentioned in his writings: as a model of chastity in the most difficult dangers of preserving virginity[99] and as a martyr of chastity.[100]

For centuries, numerous devotees of St. Thomas, who have been inspired by his exalted example, have seen and tasted how sweet the Lord is in a life that is pure, virginal, and wholly dedicated to God. In connection with spotless chastity and virginity, we have noticed in the testimonies of the canonization process the moderation and mortification of the saint regarding food and drink, his vigils, and, in general, his indifference to the pleasures and comforts of the body because of his pure love of God and inclination toward the contemplative life. St. Thomas likewise brings out, in his opusculum *De Perfectione Vitae*

Spiritualis, that those who wish to lead a pure, virginal life, in which they can more freely and perfectly dedicate themselves and cling to God, must chastise their body by fasts, vigils, and similar practices.[101]

The desires of the flesh are tamed and brought to rest through chastity and virginity, through an abstemious, austere, and mortified life, and all the pleasures of sense are willingly sacrificed for a more facile operation of the intellectual and spiritual life. At the same time, humility and its related virtues of obedience, meekness, kindness, and Christian demeanor, of amiability and friendliness, of an unselfish courtesy, bring to rest the inner concupiscences of the soul that spring from inordinate self-love, self-seeking, and the desire for honors, and, motivated by the supernatural power of charity, subordinate the whole spiritual life to God and His service. Thus man feels and finds himself fortunately in the position that is his according to the will of God and that circumstances and authority show him. He experiences in his soul the truth of our Lord's words: "Learn of me for I am meek and humble of heart, and you shall find rest to your souls" (Matt. 11:29).

We have heard how humility, meekness, obedience, and the friendly, warm, serene, and willing disposition of our saint were praised in the testimonies of the canonization process. The biography of William of Tocco also strikingly portrays the beautiful traits that humanly introduce Thomas to us as a humble, modest, peaceful, and impartial thinker, mastering all anxiety even in the face of disappointment and opposition. He remained clear and well-balanced, at all times an amiable and self-sacrificing saint and scholar. He saw in pride and arrogance an impediment to a profound grasp of truth, while in humility he beheld an aid and advancement to true wisdom. Thus, he could confess to his inseparable friend and companion, Reginald of Piperno, in all simplicity and uprightness of heart: "I give thanks to God that I have never been moved by vain glory in regard to my knowledge, my master's chair, and my public disputations.... And even though I had temptations to vain glory, I repressed them by a subsequent judgment of reason."

The testimonies of the canonization process and the canonization bull of John XXII proudly state that Thomas maintained a complete equilibrium of soul, never making use of proud or offending words during the disputations into which much excitement and haughty, proud manners frequently made their way. Bartholomew of Capua bears witness in his testimony at the process of canonization that he had heard from trustworthy Friars

Preachers how Thomas, when vehemently attacked during a disputation at Paris by the Franciscan theologian and later archbishop of Canterbury John Peckham, did not lose his self-control through proud and injurious expressions. Rather, he quietly and impartially expounded his thesis and answered in a loving and humble manner.[102] John Peckham, who wrote about this incident in an entirely different manner in a letter dated June 1, 1285, to the bishop of Lincoln, cannot help but designate Thomas as the *Doctor humilis.*[103]

Thomas also constantly remained modest and kind in his scholastic polemics, always considerate of his learned opponents.[104] Other scholastics of his time, I mention only Roger Bacon, Peter of Trabes, and Peter John Olivi, have frequently let themselves be overpowered by sharp language in scholastic encounters.

Pope Benedict XIV notes this peculiarity of St. Thomas's polemics:

> St. Thomas Aquinas, angelic leader of the Schools and Doctor of the Church, in writing so many volumes which can never be sufficiently praised, necessarily offended various opinions of philosophers and theologians which truth compelled him to refute. But

> what most admirably crowns the merits of this Doctor is that he never minimized, railed, or dishonored his opponents, but endeared all by his courtesy and friendliness. If he saw something in their writings rather harsh, ambiguous, and obscure, he explained and toned it down by a benign and lenient interpretation. If, however, for the sake of religion and faith, he was required to reject and refute their opinions, this he did with such modesty that he deserves as much praise for disagreeing as for asserting Catholic truth.[105]

Only in the work *De Unitate Intellectus Contra Averroistas*, written against Latin Averroism at the University of Paris and its leader, the shrewd philosopher Siger de Brabant, does Thomas express himself in a harsh manner against Averroes, whom he calls the *depravator* and not the *commentator* of Aristotle. He also opposes the Parisian Averroists, to whom he addresses the following rebuke near the close of his work:

> These things, therefore, we wrote to destroy the error (Averroistic Monopsychism) which is based not on the documents of faith, but on the thoughts and principles of the philosophers. If someone, glorying under the name of false

> science, wishes to say something against what we have written, let him speak not in some corner nor before children who are unable to judge in these difficult matters. Rather let him, if he so dares, write against this our tract. Then he will find not only myself, the least of them all, but many others, cultivators of truth, who can resist his error or counsel his ignorance.

I have discovered in a Munich manuscript the commentary of Siger de Brabant on a large portion of the Aristotelian works (Clm. 9559). Fr. Van Steenberghen, who, with his students, has prepared a standard edition of these questions on Aristotle, has given a very realistic picture of the philosophical doctrine and even the errors of this leader of Latin Averroism, or better, heterodoxical Aristotelianism. He has also furnished from the commentary on the *De Anima*, contained in this manuscript, the convincing proof of my opinion that Siger de Brabant had taken a different scientific position due to the weight of the proofs set forth in the work *De Unitate Intellectus*, and gave up the Averroistic Monopsychism that he previously held. We will not go far astray if we see in the humble, objective, and tender disposition of St. Thomas a reason for this intellectual realization and conversion.

This harmony, balance, and divine peace of the interior and exterior life of St. Thomas manifests itself in his prayer.[106] In the prayer after Holy Communion, the saint tenderly implores that the sacramental union with the Body and Blood of our Savior may be for him: "The extinction of vices, evil desires and concupiscences; an increase of charity and patience, of humility and obedience . . . the perfect quieting of all the inclinations of the body as well as of the soul. May it closely unite me to Thee the true and one God, and happily establish me at the end of my life in unchangeable bliss."

In other prayers of his that we have, this longing after a peaceful and harmoniously ordered inner life, clinging totally to God, manifests itself to us. In the prayer beginning *Concede mihi, misericors Deus*, which the Angelic Doctor was daily accustomed to recite before the image of the Crucified for a prudent ordering and formation of his life, he directed the following intimate plea to God:

> Grant, O Lord my God, that I may not fail in prosperity or adversity, avoiding pride in the former and discouragement in the latter. May I rejoice in nothing but what leads to Thee, and grieve for nothing but what turns away

> from Thee. May I despise, O Lord, all transitory things, and prize only that which is eternal. May I shun any joy that is not Thee; may I wish for nothing outside of Thee.... Grant me, O my God, to direct my heart toward Thee, constantly to grieve for my sins, and to amend my life. Make me, O Lord, my God, obedient without contradiction, poor without depression, chaste without corruption, patient without murmuring, humble without pretense, cheerful without dissipation ... serious without constraint, prompt without levity, God-fearing without presumption, truthful without ambiguity, eager in good works without arrogance, correcting my neighbor without haughtiness and edifying him by work and example without hypocrisy. Give me, O Lord God, a watchful heart, which no curious thought will turn away from Thee; a noble heart, which no unworthy affection will drag down; a righteous heart, which no irregular intention will turn aside; a firm heart, which no tribulation will crush; a free heart, which no violent affection will claim for its own.

His prayer for the attainment of all the virtues proceeds according to a similar train of thought. From it, I will extract only one petition, which permits us to recognize his noble, considerate disposition. He prays that he may "be troublesome to no one in bodily cares."

His prayer to the most blessed Virgin Mary is very beautiful. From this, I would like to take a few thoughts. The saint begins: "Dearest and most blessed Virgin Mary, gracious Mother of God, Daughter of the Sovereign King, Queen of the Angels, Mother of Him Who created all things, I commend to the bosom of thy mercy this day and all the days of my life, my soul, and my body, all my actions, thoughts, wishes, desires, words and deeds, my whole life and the end thereof, so that through thy prayers all may be ordered according to the will of thy beloved Son, our Lord Jesus Christ."

The saint then implores Mary's intercession for the individual attainment of all graces and virtues, which are necessary for him for a holy life in the religious state:

> Deign to implore for me from thy beloved Son, our Lord Jesus Christ, sufficient grace that I may energetically resist the temptations of the world, of the flesh, and of the evil spirit. I firmly resolve not to commit sin in the future and to persevere in thy service and in that of thy beloved Son. Most blessed

> Lady, I beseech thee to obtain for me perfect obedience and true humility of heart, so that I may truly acknowledge myself as a worthless creature and wretched sinner, unable to do any good work, or resist temptations without the grace and help of my Creator and of thy holy prayers. Procure for me also through thy prayers, O my dearest Lady, perpetual chastity of mind and body, enable me to serve thy beloved Son and thee with a pure heart and chaste body. Obtain for me from Him the grace to accept voluntary poverty with patience and serenity of mind, that I may be able to endure the burdens of this Order and work out my salvation and that of my fellowmen. Obtain for me also, O my sweetest Lady, real charity that I may love thy most holy Son, our Lord Jesus Christ, with all my heart, and next to Him, my neighbor in God and for God, and so enjoy what is good and be grieved at what is evil; grant that I may disregard no one, judge no one unkindly, nor prefer myself to anyone.

Thus the interior and exterior life of St. Thomas bears the imprint of harmony, symmetry, and balance. L. Lavaud,[107] who has given such an excellent analysis of the sanctity of

Aquinas, remarks that the moral virtues, poverty, chastity, obedience, and humility standing in the service of charity, disposed the saint for the contemplative life of divine love and wisdom. The state of original justice, order, and peace of the faculties and activities of the soul were, in a certain manner, restored in his soul. All the noblest virtues were subordinated to divine love, and all the noblest gifts of the Holy Ghost were subordinated to the gift of wisdom in his life as also in his teaching.

This harmony, symmetry, and order of the interior and exterior life, this multiplicity of virtues within the unity of love, enlightened by the light of reason, of faith, and of the gifts of the Holy Ghost, give to the soul of St. Thomas a spiritual, Godlike beauty. In one place, he has defined spiritual and intellectual beauty: *Pulchritudo spiritualis animae in hoc consistit, quod conversatio sive actio hominis sit bene proportionata secundum spiritualem rationis claritatem.*[108] The intellectual and supernatural beauty of the soul is seen in the fine proportion of life and action, which reveal harmony and symmetry in conformity with the clarity of the intellect supernaturally enlightened through faith. With this, St. Thomas has, in a certain sense, defined his own inner life.

Just as the beauty of the heavens and the splendor of the sun are reflected by a quiet flowing brook and also penetrate within, so something of the uncreated beauty of God is reflected toward us from the interior life of St. Thomas, who in the contemplation of God found the beatitude of his life.

CHAPTER 3

Christ and the Interior Life of St. Thomas

NOW WE PLAINLY SEE from the acts of the canonization process as well as from his writings how wisdom, charity, and peace stand out as the basic features of St. Thomas's soul.

From this portrait of his soul and character radiates the meek and peaceful splendor of his wisdom, love, and peace in Christ Jesus in all its fullness. We can thoroughly understand the interior life of St. Thomas, like that of any other saint, only when we see this inner life and love related to Christ.

William of Tocco has embodied in his biography of St. Thomas the well-known account of the saint's mystical experience in the chapel of St. Nicholas, in the Dominican Church S. Domenico Maggiore at Naples.[109] The sacristan, a lay-Brother, Dominic of Caserta, beheld St. Thomas in ecstasy before the image of the Crucified. He heard the words from the mouth of the age-old crucifix: "You have written well of me, Thomas; what reward do you wish for your labors?" He then heard the reply: "Nothing less than you, O Lord," come from the lips of the saint. Thereupon, William of Tocco remarks, St. Thomas wrote the third part of his *Summa*, which treats of the Passion and Resurrection of Christ.[110]

Art has frequently portrayed this scene of Christian mysticism. We see it at the Vatican art gallery in a portrait by the Sienese painter Stefano di Giovanni, known as Sassetta, in an altar painting by the Spanish artist Berruguete[111] exhibited in the Prado Museum at Madrid, and last, in the cycle of mural paintings on the life of St. Thomas in the Dominican Church at Regensburg, publicized and explained by J. A. Endres.[112] The latest and most impressive portrayal of this vision is the beautiful painting by Martin Feuerstein.

Christ is, for Thomas, the origin and sum total of all wisdom. None of the great theologians of the Middle Ages has written more profoundly than Thomas on either the infinite divine wisdom of the Eternal Word or on the wisdom of Christ's human soul hypostatically united to the Logos. The 216th chapter of his *Compendium Theologiae*, "The Plenitude of Christ's Wisdom," condenses with inimitable clarity and profundity into one lucid presentation whatever the great theologian has detailed in his larger works on Christology.

In the Incarnation of Jesus Christ, St. Thomas sees and admires the greatest act of God's wisdom. He seeks with all the power of his mind and all the love of his heart to penetrate into the theology of this mystery. Whatever he has written on the purposefulness of the Incarnation in both his *Summae* is both speculative and contemplative, scholastic and mystic. In the fourth book of the *Summa contra Gentiles*, the fifty-third chapter, the saint begins his masterful presentation with words written from his own intimate experience: "If anyone would diligently and piously consider the mysteries of the Incarnation, he would find such a profundity of wisdom that it would exceed all human knowledge, according to the words of the Apostle: 'The foolishness of God is wiser than men.' Wherefore the wonderful meaning (*rationes*) of this mystery is manifested more and more to him who piously ponders it."

For St. Thomas, Christ is the source of all wisdom. Union with Christ permits us to participate in His wisdom and makes us truly wise. In his explanation of the passage: "of Christ Jesus, in whom are hidden all the treasures of wisdom and knowledge" (Col. 2:3), Thomas draws this practical conclusion: "Therefore we must seek wisdom nowhere else except in Christ ... just as he who had a book which contained wisdom would not seek to know anything except this book. Thus we should never seek anything more than Christ."[113]

As much as Thomas treasured the profane natural sciences so as to devote a large part of his literary activity to explaining Aristotle's writings, and as little as he shared in the harsh attitude of earlier and contemporary theologians, narrow-minded and fearful of philosophy and human knowledge,[114] he nevertheless placed truth revealed to us in Christ far above all this human science and wisdom. He writes at the beginning of his explanation to the Creed: "Despite all their efforts, none of the philosophers before Christ could have known about God and the truths necessary for eternal life so much as a simple woman knows through faith after the advent of Christ." In a sermon that he delivered about the year 1270 at the University of Paris,[115] he expressed himself in much the same way: "A simple woman now knows more about the truths of faith than all philosophers will ever know."

To be immersed in the humanity of Jesus Christ is the way that leads to a knowledge of His Divinity. The Augustinian thought—through Christ the man to Christ the God[116]—also vividly appears in Thomas. In his *Compendium Theologiae*, he writes these striking words: "The humanity of Christ is the way by which we come to the divinity."[117] This is the basic idea of Christian mysticism. Henry Suso, for example, in his *Book of Wisdom* places on the lips of the Eternal Wisdom the words: "If you wish to behold me in my eternal divinity, you must learn to know and love me in my suffering humanity."[118] The Benedictine mystic from Bavaria, John of Castel,[119] always faithful to Thomas, thoroughly understood, felt, and developed in his book *De adhaerendo Deo*—and even more beautifully and profoundly in the yet unpublished work *De Lumine Increato*—this thought: that the created light of Christ's humanity ought to lead us, detached as far as possible from earthly affections, to the very heights of human love and experience, the contemplation of the uncreated light of the divinity.

The Cross of our Savior is for Thomas the unique source of wisdom and the hearth of his glowing love of God and Christ. Thus we come naturally to the consideration of the second basic feature in the interior life of St. Thomas, to charity with its devotedness to Christ. Here, knowledge and love unite most intimately. A. Touron, O.P., remarks so beautifully:

> The Cross of the Saviour was his first book, the great object of his meditations, the rule of his whole life. At the feet of the Cross he humbled his spirit to merit an understanding of the mysteries of faith; he purified his heart

> to render himself capable of receiving it. There he learned the secret of penetrating into truth by way of charity, and of basing all his knowledge on that of Jesus Christ, of himself, and of his salvation. There those untimely distractions, which so often make us sigh ... almost never interrupted this happy intercourse where his heart unfolded itself in thanksgiving, and his soul, always attentive to the voice of God, listened in silence to what the Eternal Word wished to make known to him. This eternal wisdom that the Apostle learned in the third heaven, the beloved disciple on the breast of the Saviour, and St. Augustine in Holy Writ, St. Thomas learned at the feet of the crucifix. The wounds of Jesus Christ were the masters whom he consulted in his doubts and to whom he listened in his difficulties.... From this source he drew the principles of his science, the abundance and purity of his doctrine.[120]

In the Cross, St. Thomas beheld "the perfection of the whole law, and the complete art of living well."[121]

Reflection on the mysteries and deeds of the most sacred humanity of Jesus Christ awakens devotion and inflames love. This reflection on the divinity and whatever pertains to it, the Angelic Doctor brings out, is in itself most fit to enkindle our charity and arouse our devotion since God, in truth, must be loved above all. However, because of our weakness of spirit, we need support and direction from objects appealing to the senses for our love of God just as we do for our knowledge of God. Thus the humanity of Jesus Christ takes the first place in our consideration, as is mentioned in the preface for Christmas: "*Ut dum visibiliter Deum cognoscimus per hunc in invisibilium amorem rapiamur*" (So that while we acknowledge God in visible form, we may through Him be drawn to the love of things invisible). Whatever, therefore, immediately refers to the humanity of Jesus Christ is especially fit to lead us, as it were, by the hand to interior devotion and charity. Nevertheless, the primary object of our devotion remains the divinity itself.[122]

From his immersion into the most holy life of Jesus Christ, St. Thomas also assimilated that peace of soul, which from the imitation of Christ springs into a harmonious practice of the Christian virtues, warmed and enlightened by charity. A priceless treasure of thought on the incomparably sublime and ineffably beautiful example of virtue in the God-man, and on the practical imitation of Christ, lies hidden in his commentaries on the

Scriptures, and in his profound questions in the third part of the *Summa*, which treat of the mysteries of the life, Passion, death, and Resurrection of Christ. The meditative and contemplative insight of the saint is focused upon the minutest detail as well as upon the whole of our Savior's exterior and interior life. It finds particular joy in the harmony of this most sacred inner life, in which no sounds of discord can be heard.

Omnis Christi actio nostra est instructio (every action of Christ is a lesson for us). This thought frequently recurs in St. Thomas. In the divine work of Christ, he perceives the exemplar of the effects of divine grace in us. The activity of the most sacred humanity shows us how we should cooperate with the grace of God.[123] The saint places special stress upon both the example and the imitation of the obedience of Christ, who died for us out of love and obedience to His heavenly Father. "In this [Christ] gave an example—that just as He renounced His human will by submitting it to the divine, so we also should submit our will totally to God and to men who are placed over us as God's ministers."[124]

His exposition of the virtuous life of Christ reveals the precision of His basic dogmatic thoughts. The dogma of the hypostatic union, grasped so profoundly by Thomas, appears in the psychology of Jesus Christ, as he paints it with the colors of Holy Writ and the Fathers. The fanciful imagination, which in the mysticism of the Bonaventurian school has created the meditations on Christ's life by John of Caulas, never or very seldom comes into play in Aquinas's portrait of Christ.

The deep and pious disposition of the saint comes to the fore in a very attractive manner in some of his smaller works where he depicts the Divine Savior as the model of virtue. From these we sense what the saint has thought and felt about Christ in his studies, meditations, and prayers—what he drew from them to fashion his own interior life. I believe that a few texts from St. Thomas's mysticism on Christ and His Passion will also introduce us to the dispositions and feelings of his inner life so completely imbued with Christ.[125]

In his comprehensive exposition on the Creed, Thomas explains for our everyday life the significance of each article of faith. From the doctrine of faith that the only-begotten Word is of the same nature with the Father, he deduces the practical conclusions "*ad consolationem nostram*" (for our consolation), as he expresses it: "If the Word of God is the Son of God, and all the words of God have a certain likeness to this Word, we first ought to hear gladly the words of God ... to believe the words of God ... to meditate constantly upon the word of God ... to communicate the word of God to others by admonishing, preaching, and enkindling ... and to put the word of God into practice."

From the Incarnation of the Son of God: "*homo factus est*" (He became man), the holy Doctor likewise offers some practical applications for our learning: "From these mysteries our faith is confirmed, our hope elevated, our charity inflamed. We are incited to keep our love pure by thoughts on the dignity bestowed upon human nature from the Incarnation. By meditating upon the Incarnation of the Son of God, we are eventually filled with a holy desire to belong to Christ."

The treatise on Christ as the model of virtue in His Passion and death is exceptionally beautiful:

> For if you seek an example of charity, greater charity no man has than that he give up his life for his friends—and this Christ did upon the Cross. So if He gave His life for us, it should not be difficult for us to suffer many hardships for Him.... If you seek an example of patience, the most excellent is found upon the Cross where Jesus freely underwent the greatest sufferings with the most heroic patience.... If you

> seek an example of humility, behold the Crucified, for God desired to be condemned and die under Pontius Pilate—the Lord for the servant, the life of the Angels for *man*.... If you seek an example of obedience, follow Him Who was obedient to the Father even unto death.... If you seek an example of despising earthly goods, follow Him Who is King of kings, Lord of lords, in Whom are all the treasures of wisdom. Upon the Cross, however, He was naked, mocked, spat upon, scourged, crowned with thorns, given vinegar and gall to drink, and crucified. Do not therefore become too much attached to clothing or to riches, for they have divided my vesture among themselves. Do not desire honors, for I have suffered insults and lashes. Do not seek dignities, for they have placed a crown of thorns upon my head. Do not revel in delicacies, for they have quenched my thirst with gall.

The same thoughts on the mysticism of Christ and His Passion are also found in another opusculum of St. Thomas. The opusculum directed against Nicholas of Lisieux in 1270, *Contra pestiferam doctrinam retrahentium homines a religionis ingressu*, begins with an exposition of the idea of imitating the humble and poor Jesus. The Angelic Doctor states:

> The purpose of the Christian religion seems to consist principally in this—that men withdraw from earthly things and become intent upon things spiritual. Hence it was that Jesus, the author and consummator of faith, by His entry into the world showed His faithful in word and deed contempt for temporal affairs.... He was born of a mother, who, although untouched by man at conception and during life, nevertheless was espoused to a carpenter—thus He excluded any form of carnal nobility. He was born in the town of Bethlehem, which was insignificant among the cities of Judea—thus He did not wish anyone to glory in the grandeur of a terrestrial city. He who possessed all and through whom all things are, became poor, lest anyone, believing in Him, would dare to boast of worldly riches. He did not wish to be made king, for He pointed out the way of humility. He, who fed all, hungered; He, who created all drink, thirsted; He, who opened up the way to Heaven, grew tired on His journey; He, who ended our afflictions, was crucified; He, who awakened the dead, died for man.

The opusculum *De Rationibus Fidei contra Saracenos, Graecos et Armenos ad Cantorem Antiochenum*,[126] also translated into Greek, is filled with beautiful and profound thoughts on Christ's sacred life and example of virtue, and, in general, on the ascetical and mystical significance of the doctrine of the Incarnation. It is a genuine treasure of the beauty and clarity of St. Thomas's theological thought.

I am extracting a few thoughts from the seventh chapter of this truly valuable work, which treats of Christ's Passion and death:

> If anyone considers from a pious motive the fitness of the passion and death of Christ, he will find such a profundity of knowledge that continuously more and greater thoughts come to him.... The first consideration is that Christ assumed our human nature to repair the fall of man. Therefore it was necessary that Christ suffer and do those things according to His human nature which could offer a remedy for sin. The sin of man consists in his clinging to corporal things, leaving aside spiritual goods. It befitted the Son of God therefore in His assumed human nature to show by His deeds and sufferings that men should despise temporal goods and evil, lest being impeded by an inordinate affection for them, they

should be less given to spiritual things. Thus Christ chose parents who were poor, yet perfected in virtue, so that nobody would glory solely in nobility of flesh and wealth of parents. He led the life of a poor man that He might teach us to despise riches. He lived without honors that He might restrain men from seeking them inordinately. He underwent labor, hunger, thirst, and a scourging of the body, lest men, intent upon pleasures and luxuries, be drawn away from the good of virtue because of the difficulties of life. Ultimately He underwent death, lest anybody might deny the truth because of the fear of death. And so that nobody would fear to suffer a horrible death for truth, He chose the most despicable type of death—that of the cross. Thus it was fitting for the Son of God made man to suffer death, so that by His example He might incite men to virtue.

Not only virtuous conduct is necessary for men to attain salvation ... but also a knowledge of truth.... Therefore it was necessary that the Son of God made man give to men a doctrine of divine truth. And to prove this truth to be divine and not human, He wrought a great number of miracles.

In the humility, poverty, and lowliness of Jesus Christ, St. Thomas finds strength and confirmation to prove His miracles:

> If Christ had lived in wealth, power, and great dignity, it could be believed that His doctrine and miracles had been received by reason of human ingenuity and favour. And so that the work might manifestly be of divine power, He chose what was abject and lowly in the world: a poor mother and a needy life, uneducated Apostles and disciples; to be despised by the great men of the world, and eventually to be condemned to death. In this way He manifestly showed that the acceptance of His miracles and of His doctrine ought to be attributed to divine rather than human power.
>
> Therefore in all that He accomplished and suffered, human infirmity is simultaneously conjoined with divine power. In His nativity, wrapped up in swaddling clothes, He was placed in a manger—but gloriously praised by angels and adored by the Magi. He was tempted by the devil, but ministered to by angels. He lived in need and poverty, but raised the dead to life and gave sight to the blind. He died fixed to a Cross, numbered among thieves, but at His death the sun was

> darkened, the earth trembled, the stones were shattered, the graves were opened, and the bodies of the dead arose. If, therefore, from such a beginning, one sees the fruit which followed, namely the conversion of nearly the whole world to Christ, and still seeks other signs for believing, he can be regarded as harder than a rock, for at His death the rocks burst asunder.

Such is St. Thomas's devotion to Christ. His whole interior life is illumined by the dogmatic notion of the God-man and His work of Redemption, all of which he understood so deeply. His innermost wishes and strivings glow with a deep love of Christ. His life and actions are fashioned and transfigured by an everyday imitation of Christ. Consequently, his life in Christ constitutes the ultimate reason for his wisdom, love, and peace—the essential traits in the interior life of St. Thomas.

St. Thomas's whole intellectual life is determined and oriented from above. He hopes for and obtains true wisdom from the heavenly heights, toward which his intellect gazes with ardor and faith. Thither he lifts himself upon the wings of charity, which contemplates and loves God in all things. From these heights, that peace flows into his soul, which the world cannot give, which Christ brought into the world and diffuses in those who are docile.

St. Thomas impressively proclaimed his ideal understanding of his academic and scientific life's work in a recently discovered inaugural address, which he delivered when he was installed in the office of Master of Theology at the University of Paris in 1256.[127]

It begins with the words of Psalm 103, verse 13: "Thou waterest the hills from thy upper rooms: the earth shall be filled with the fruits of thy works." Just as the mountains tower high above the earth and are near the heavens, in like manner the doctors of truth must rise above the things of this earth and strive only after heavenly things. Just as the mountains are first illumined by the light from the sun, so also the doctors of sacred science receive the splendor of the mind first (*mentium splendorem prius recipiant*). Their intellectual life participates in eternity (*qui sunt in participatione aeternitatis*).

He concludes this profound inaugural address with the biblical thought that God generously gives to all who implore Him for wisdom, and then adds:

"Let us pray, that God grant it to us all. Amen."

Endnotes

1 Guilio Bertoni, ed. Emilio Paolo Vicini, *Tommaso da Modena. Atti e Memorie della R. Deputazione di storia patria per le provincie modenesi,* serie V, vol. 3, 1904. J. J. Berthier, O.P., *Le Chapitre de San Niccolo de Trevise. Peintures de fra Tommaso da Modena* (Rome, 1912).

2 Paolo D'Ancona, *Le miniature fiorentine* (sec. XI–XV), II (Firenze, 1914), p. 487.

3 Cf. M. Grabmann, *Neuaufgefundene Werke deutscher Mystiker. Sitzungsberichte der Bayerischen Akademie der Wissenschaften.* Philosoph.—philol. und hist. Klasse (München, 1922), p. 18.

4 Cf. L. Lavaud, *Saint Thomas "Guide des Études." Notes et commentaires sur L'Encyclique Studiorum ducem de* S. S. *Pie XI* (Paris, 1925).

5 A. Touron, O.P., *La vie de S. Thomas d'Aquin* (Paris, 1737), pp. 373–592.

6 M. Gillet, O.P., *La personnalité de Saint Thomas et l'impersonnalité de sa doctrine* (Toulouse, 1919). H. Petitot, O.P., *Saint Thomas d'Aquin* (2 ed.) (Paris, 1923). S. Ramirez, O.P., "Qué es un tomista?" *La Ciencia tomista,* 1920 (pp. 166–180 give a very striking analysis of the scientific individuality of St. Thomas). G.M. Manser, O.P., "Die wissenschaftliche Persönliclikeit des hl. Thomas von Aquin," *Divus Thomas,* 1923, pp. 218–232. Cf. also P. Rouselot, S.J., "L'esprit de Saint Thomas," *Etudes,* 1911, pp. 614–629. B. Jansen, S.J., "Die wissenschaftliche Eigenart des

Aquinaten," *Stimmen der Zeit,* 98 (1920), pp. 442–456. B. Jansen, S.J., *Wege der Weltweisheit* (Freiburg, 1924), pp. 98–124. Other contributions that offer a picture of the soul and character of St. Thomas are: *Saint Thomas, Études publiées par le College Dominicain d'Ottawa à l'occasion de sa Canonisation* (Ottawa, 1923). M. Cordovani, O.P., *L'attualità di* S. *Tommaso d'Aquino* (Milano, 1923). R. Fei, O.P., *San Tommaso d'Aquino, L'Uomo, Il Domenicano, Il Santo, Il Genio* (Torino, 1923). R.M. Giuliani, O.P., *L'Angelo delle Scuole* (Torino, 1924). M. Jacquin, O.P., *Le "Prudentissime Frère Thomas,"* Conférence (Fribourg, 1924). J. Maritain, "Saint Thomas, apôtre des temps modernes," *Revue des Jeunes,* XIV (1924), pp. 461–505.

7 A. D. Sertillanges, O.P., *St. Thomas Aquinas and His Work,* trans. Godfrey Anstruther, O.P. (London: Burns, Oates and Washbourne, Ltd., 1932). J. Webert, O.P., *Saint Thomas d'Aquin. Le génie de l'ordre* (Paris, 1934). Th. Deman, O.P., "La sainteté de Saint Thomas d'Aquin," *La vie spirituelle,* 42 (1935), Supp. (129–180). J.E. Kuiper, *Thomas van Aquino de Heilige* (Amsterdam, 1927). G. Salvadori, *Il cuore, il buon senso, e il genio di S. Tomaso* (Arezzo, 1929). J. Pieper, *Über Thomas von Aquin* (Leipzig, 1940). A. Walz, O.P., *San Tommaso d'Aquino, Studi biografici* (Roma, 1944). M. Grabmann, *Thomas Aquinas, His Personality and Thought,* trans. Virgil Michel, O.S.B. (New York: Longmans, Green and Co., 1928).

8 For the canonization process of St. Thomas, cf. P. Mandonnet, O.P., *La canonisation de Saint Thomas d'Aquin* (18 *juillet,* 1323). *Extrait des Melanges Thomistes publiées à l'occasion du VI6 Centenaire,* Le Saulchoir Kain, (Belgique), 1923. A. Gigon, O.P., "Histoire de la canonisation de Saint Thomas d'Aquin," *Revue Thomiste,* 1923, pp. 142 ff., 261 ff. M. Grabmann, "Die Kanonisation des hl. Thomas von Aquin in ihrer Bedeutung für die Ausbreitung und Verteidigung seiner Lehre im 14. Jahrhundert," *Divus Thomas,* 1923, pp. 233–249. A. Walz, O.P., *Canonizationis S. Thomae de*

Aquino brevis historia (Romae, 1924). *Fontes vitae* S. *Thomae Aquinatis* cura et labore M.–H. Laurent, O.P., IV. Processus *canonizationis* S. *Thomae Neapoli,* 1934. V. *Processus canonizationis S. Thomae Fossae Novae* (Documents inédits par la *Revue Thomiste*) (Saint Maximin, 1937). Since this publication was not at my disposal, I had to use the *Acta Sanctorum.*

9 I. Taurisano, O.P., "Discepoli e biografi di S. Tommaso. S. Tommaso d'Aquino," *Miscellanea storico-artistica* (Roma, 1924), pp. 11–186.

10 For this letter cf. M. Grabmann, "Werke des hl. Thomas von Aquin. Eine literar-historische Untersuchung und Einführung" (2 ed.), (*Beiträge zur Geschichte der Philosophie des Mittelalters,* herausgegeben von Cl. Baeumker, XXII, 1–2) (Münster, 1931), p. 300.

11 P. Castagnoli, *L'opusculo De forma absolutionis di San Tommaso d'Aquino,* Seconda edizione (Piacenza, 1933). L. Ott, "Das opusculum des hl. Thomas von Aquin De forma absolutionis in dogmengeschichtlicher Betrachtung," *Festschrift Eichmann* (Paderborn, 1940), pp. 99–135.

12 J. Destrez, "La lettre de S. Thomas d'Aquin dite lettre au lecteur de Venise, d'après la traduction manuscrite," *Mélanges Mandonnet,* I (Paris, 1930), pp. 103–189.

13 For this writing cf. M. Grabmann, "Die Werke des hl. Thomas von Aquin," p. 299.

14 *Acta Sanctorum,* Martii, tom. I, p. 699.

15 Ibid., p. 700.

16 Ibid., p. 701.

17 Ibid., p. 705 f.

18 For John Regina of Naples, cf. M. Grabmann, *Mittelalterliches Geistesleben,* I (München, 1926), pp. 374–384. J. Taurisano, O.P., *op. cit.,* pp. 51–55, 73 f. Th. Kaeppeli, O.P., "Note sugli scrittori domenicani di nome Giovanni di Napoli," *Archivum Fratrum Praedicatorum,* 10 (1940), pp. 48–71.

19 *Acta Sanctorum,* Martii, tom. I, p. 701.

20 Ibid., p. 711 ff.

21 A photostat of the original bull of canonization, retained in the Archives départementales de la Haute-Garonne at Toulouse under the title Série H. Dominicains, liasse 99, is included in a series of writings on the occasion of St. Thomas's canonization jubilee: in the excellent work by P.L. Ferretti, O.P., *In honorem D. Thomae Aquinatis sexto saeculo exeunte a sanctorum caelitum honoribus ipsi decretis Documenta Pontificia miris artis operibus illustrata* (Romae, 1923); in the festival number of *Divus Thomas* (3. Heft, 1923); in the large and profound *Xenia Thomistica* (Romae, 1924); edited by P. S. Szabò, O.P. Angelus Walz, O.P., archivist of the general archives of the Dominican Order in Rome, has edited the canonization bull in the *Analecta Ordinis Praedicatorum* (Aug. Vol., 1923), which is based on a thorough historical and diplomatic research. It also appears separately under the title *De Bulla Canonizationis Sancti Thomae Aquinatis* (Romae, 1923).

22 L. Ferretti, *In honorem D. Thomae Aquinatis sexto saeculo exeunte a sanctorum caelitum honoribus ipsi decretis Documenta Pontificia miris artis operibus illustrata* (Romae, 1923), tab. VIII, p. 73.

23 Ibid., tab. IX, p. 74.

24 J.J. Berthier, O.P., Le *triomphe de Saint Thomas peint par Taddeo Gaddi dans la chapelle des Espagnols à Florence* (Fribourg [Suisse], 1897), p. 56. B.H. Molkenboer, O.P., *De spansche Kapel de Florence,* Overdruk uit Van onzen Tijd Jaargang (1911–1912). B.H. Molkenboer, O.P., "Der hl. Thomas van Aquino in de Schilderkunst," in: A.W. Winckel, O.P., en E. Van Goethem, *San Thomas van Aquino.* Bijdragen over zijn Tijd, zijn Leer en zijn Verheerlijking dor de Kunst (Gent, 1927), pp. 143–223, speziell pp. 158–160. L. Gillet, *Histoire artistique des Ordres mendiants* (Paris, 1912), pp. 137–152.

25 R. Garrigou-Lagrange, O.P., *God: His Existence and His Nature,* trans. Dom. Bede Rose, O.S.B. (Herder Book Co., 1934).

26 Fr. Olgiati, *The Key to the Study of St. Thomas,* trans. John S. Zybura, Ph.D. (St. Louis: B. Herder, 1929).

27 M. Grabmann, *Der göttliche Grund der menschlichen Wahrheitserkenntnis nach Augustinus und Thomas von Aquin* (Münster, 1924).

28 Cf. R. Garrigou-Lagrange, O.P., "De spiritu supernaturali Theologiae D. Thomae," *Miscellanea Dominicana* (Romae, 1923), pp. 141–150. Gilson, *The Philosophy of St. Thomas Aquinas,* trans. Edward Bullough, M.A., ed. G.A. Elrington, O.P., D.Sc., 3 ed. (Herder Book Co., 1941), pp. 37–54. G.M. Manser, O.P., *Das Wesen des Thomismus,* "Die aristotelische Lehre von Akt und Potenz als Grundlage der thomistischen Fassung von Glaube und Wissen," 3 ed. (Freiburg, 1949), pp. 114–139.

29 H. Meyer, *The Philosophy of St. Thomas Aquinas,* trans. Rev. Frederic Eckhoff (Herder Book Co., 1945). P. Wyser, O.P., *Thomas von Aquin, In librum Boethii de Trinitate quaestiones quinta et sexta.* Published according to the Autograph Cod. Vat. lat. 9850 with an introduction (Fribourg-Louvain, 1948).

30 To the metaphysics of St. Thomas see L. De Raeymaeker, *Metaphysica generalis* (Louvain, 1931). F. Van Steenberghen, *Metaphysique* (Louvain, 1931).

31 J. Reinke, *Naturwissenschaft, Weltanschauung, Religion* (Freiburg, 1923), p. 8.

32 M.D. Chenu, O.P., *La théologie comme science au XIIIe siècle,* deuxième édition, 1943. P. Wyser, O.P., *Die Theologie als Wissenschaft* (Salzburg-Leipzig, 1936). M. Grabmann, *Die theologische Erkenntnis- und Einleitungslehre des hl. Thomas von Aquin auf Grund der Schrift In Boethium de Trinitate* (in the Thomistic study series) (Freiburg in der Schweiz, 1948).

33 *In Boethium de Trinitate,* q. 2, a. 2.

34 *Summa Theologica,* I, q. 1, art. 3, ad. 2.

35 *In I Sent. prol.* a. 3, sol. 1.

36 *In Epistola ad Hebraeos,* V, lect. 2.

37 *Summa Theologica,* II–II, q. 152, art. 2.

38 *In Mattheo,* cap. 11.

39 *In Evangelio Joannis,* cap. 5, lect. 6.

40 *Summa Theologica,* II–II, q. 45, art. 2. Cf. M.J. Scheeben, *Handbuch der katholischen Dogmatik,* I, p. 410 ff. M. Grabmann, "Matthias Joseph Scheebens Auffassung vom Wesen und Wert der theologischen Wissenschaft," in: *Matthias Scheeben, Der Erneuerer katholischer Glaubenswissenschaften* (Mainz, 1935), pp. 55–108.

41 E. Van Steenberghe, "Autour de la 'Docte Ignorance.' Une controverse sur la Théologie mystique au XVe siècle" (*Beiträge zur Geschichte der Philosophic des Mittelalters,* heraugegeben von Cl. Baeumker, XIX, 2–4) (Münster, 1915), p. 208.

42 Dom C. Butler, O.S.B., *Western Mysticism* (Constable, 1922).

43 *Christian Perfection and Contemplation,* trans. Sr. M. Timothea Doyle, O.P. (St. Louis: B. Herder, 1942). *The Three Ages of the Interior Life: Prelude of Eternal Life,* trans. Sr. M. Timothea Doyle, O.P., II, (St. Louis: B. Herder, 1947 and 1948).

44 A. Gardeil, O.P., *The Gifts of the Holy Ghost in the Dominican Saints,* trans. Anselm M. Townsend, O.P. (Milwaukee: Bruce, 1942). For an understanding of the mysticism of St. Thomas, the work by A. Gardeil, O.P., *La structure de I'âme et l'expérience mystique* (Paris, 1927), is exceedingly valuable.

45 L. Lavaud, "Notes distinctives de la sainteté," *La vie spirituelle,* VIII (1923): Saint Thomas, Docteur mystique, p. 348.

46 *Acta Sanctorum, loc. cit.,* p. 712 f. Cf. A. Walz, O.P., *San Tommaso d'Aquino,* pp. 176–180.

47 L. Lavaud, "Notes distinctives de la sainteté," p. 350.

48 H.D. Lacordaire, *Mémoire pour le rétablissement en France de l'ordre des Frères Prêcheurs* (Paris, 1852), p. 82 ff.

49 From the recent rich literature concerning St. Thomas's teaching on supernatural charity and the friendship of God, the following are cited: J. Keller, O.P., "De virtute caritatis ut amicitia quadam divina," *Xenia thomistica,* II (Romae, 1925), pp. 233–276. Cardinalis J.E. Van Roey, *De virtute caritatis quaestiones selectae*

(Mechliniae, 1929). R. Garrigou-Lagrange, O.P., *The Love of God and the Cross of Jesus*, trans. Sr. Jeanne Marie, O.P. (St. Louis: B. Herder, 1947). H.D. Noble, O.P., *L'amitié avec Dieu. Essai sur la vie spirituelle d'après S. Thomas d'Aquin,* deuxième édition (Paris, 1932). P. Philippe, O.P., *Le rôle de l'amitié dans la vie chrétienne selon S. Thomas d'Aquin* (Rome, 1938). R. Egenter, *Die Lehre von der Gottesfreundschaft in der Scholastik und Mystik des 12. und* 13. *Jahrhunderts* (Augsburg, 1928), pp. 7–131. H. Wilms, O.P., *Die Gottesfreundschaft nach dem hl. Thomas* (Vechta, 1933).

50 Cf. M. Grabmann, *Wesen und Grundlagen der katholischen Mystik*, 2 ed. (Münster, 1923), 45 f.

51 *Summa Theologica,* II–II, q. 17, art. 6, ad. 3.

52 Ibid., q. 23, art. 8; q. 184, art. 2. This doctrine of St. Thomas is exposed most profoundly by Garrigou-Lagrange, O.P., *Christian Perfection and Contemplation*, trans. Sr. Timothea Doyle, O.P. (St. Louis: B. Herder, 1942), pp. 129–146. Also cf. M.A. Janvier, O.P., *Exposition de la Morale catholique, Morale spéciale,* XIII: "La Perfection dans la vie chrétienne" (Paris, 1923). Th. M. Pègues, O.P., *Commentaire francais littéral de la Somme Théologique,* XIV: "Les Etats" (Paris, 1921), p. 328 ff.

53 *Theologia mentis et cordis,* as quoted by Lavaud, "Notes distinctives de la sainteté," p. 358.

54 *De Perfectione vitae spiritualis,* cap. 6. Cf. R. Garrigou-Lagrange, O.P., *Christian Perfection and Contemplation*, p. 129 ff. O. Klingler, O.S.B., *Der Stand the christlichen Vollkommenheit nach der Lehre des hl. Thomas von Aquin* (St. Ottilien, 1926).

55 II–II, q. 185–189.

56 *De perfectione vitae spiritualis*, cap. 23.

57 Cf. M. Grabmann, *Die Kulturwerte der deutschen Mystik* (Augsburg, 1923), p. 39 f.

58 *Summa Theologica,* I–II, q. 61, art. 5.

59 *Summa Theologica,* I–II, q. 112, art. 5. Cf. the wonderful exposition on this point in A. Touron's book, *La vie de S. Thomas d'Aquin,* pp. 576–582.

60 *Summa Theologica,* II–II, q. 28.

61 Ibid., q. 82, art. 4. Cf. the beautiful commentary by A. Gardeil, O.P., "L'éducation personelle et surnaturelle de soi-même par la vertu de religion," *Revue Thomiste,* 1922, p. 14 ff.

62 *Summa Theologica,* II–II, q. 82, art. 4, ad. 3.

63 Ibid., III, q. 79, art. 8.

64 Ibid., III, q. 79, art. 1, ad. 2.

65 *In IV Sent.,* d. 12, q. 2, art. 2, s. 1, ad. 2.

66 H. Cormier, O.P., *Étude sur Saint Thomas et l'office du très saint Sacrement* (Lille, 1884). Cl. Blume, S.J., "Thomas von Aquin und das Fronleichnamsofficium, insbesondere der Hymnus Verbum supernum," *Theologie und Glaube,* III (1911), pp. 358–372. F. Trucco, *San Tommaso d'Aquino poeta della Santissima Eucharistia* (Sarzana, 1928). O. Huf, S.J., *De Sacramentshymnen von de H. Thomas van Aquino* (Maestricht, 1924). Vanhaeve, "Thomas van Aquino De Dichter," *Onze Jeugd,* 5 (1927), pp. 70–114. M. Grabmann, "Die Werke des hl. Thomas," pp. 317–321.

67 Mandonnet, O.P., *Les écrits authentiques de Saint Thomas d'Aquin,* (Fribourg [Suisse], 1910), p. 99.

68 *IV Sent., dist.* 8, q. 2, sol. 3, ad. 5m.

69 *Summa Theologica,* II–II, q. 184, art. 8.

70 J.A. Endres, *Thomas von Aquin* (Mainz, 1910), p. 69.

71 L. Ferretti, *In honorem D. Thomae Aquinatis sexto saeculo exeunte a sanctorum caelitum honoribus ipsi decretis Documenta Pontificia miris artis operibus illustrata* (Romae, 1923), tab. XII, p. 75.

72 A. Touron, O.P., *La vie de S. Thomas d'Aquin,* p. 381 f.

73 *Summa Theologica,* II–II, q. 29. Cf. F.A. Claverie, O.P., "La notion catholique de la paix," *Revue Thomiste,* 1919, pp. 125–166.

74 *Summa Theologica,* I–II, q. 69, art. 3.

75 P. Mandonnet, O.P., "Chronologie sommaire de la vie at des écrits de Saint Thomas," *Revue des sciences philosophiques et théologiques,* 1920, p. 143. H. Petitot, O.P., "La vocation de Saint Thomas d'Aquin," *La vie spirituelle,* VII (1923), p. 611 ff. A. Walz, O.P., *San Tommaso d'Aquino,* pp. 10–22. For the residence of St. Thomas at Monte Cassino cf. T. Leccisotti, "Il Dottore Angelico a Monte Cassino," *Rivista di filosofia neoscolastica,* 32 (1940), pp. 519–547.

76 R. B. Vaughan, O.S.B., *The Life and Labours of St. Thomas of Aquin* (London, 1872), I, pp. XII–XIII.

77 B. Allo, O.P., *La paix dans la vérité. Étude sur la personalité de S. Thomas d'Aquin* (Paris, 1911).

78 For this cf. especially O. Schilling, *Die Staats- und Soziallehre des hl. Thomas von Aquin* (München, 1930).

79 For this cf. M. Grabmann, *Thomas Aquinas, His Personality and Thought.*

80 In *II. Metaph.,* lect. 1.

81 A. Harnack, *Lehrbuch der Dogmengeschichte,* III (4 ed.) (Tübingen, 1910), p. 498.

82 In *I. De caelo et mundo*, lect. 22.

83 P. Duhem, *Le système du monde. Histoire des doctrines cosmologiques de Platon à Copernic,* V (Paris, 1917), pp. 468–580.

84 F. Van Steenberghen gives the best character study of the Aristotelianism of St. Thomas in his work: *Siger de Brabant d'après ses oeuvres inédites.* Second volume: *Siger dans l'histoire de l'Aristotélisme* (Louvain, 1942), pp. 479–489. M. Grabmann, "Der Aristotelismus des hl. Thomas von Aquin," *Theologie und Glaube,* 1940, pp. 19–26.

85 R. Seeberg, *Lehrbuch der Dogmengeschichte,* III (2 ed.) (Leipzig), p. 369 f.

86 Cf. M. Grabmann, *Die Lehre des hl. Thomas von Aquin von der Kirche als Gotteswerk* (Regensburg, 1903). M. J. Congar, O.P., *Esquisses du mystère de I'Église* (Paris, 1941). H. De Lubac, S.J.,

Corpus Christi mysticum, l'Eucharistie et l'Église an moyen âge (Paris, 1944).

87 *Summa Theologica,* III, q. 80, art. 11.

88 *Quodl.,* II, a. 7. Cf. *Quodl.* III, a. 10. *Summa Theologica,* I, q. 32, art. 4.

89 *De Potentia,* III, a. 18.

90 Card. Cajetanus, O.P., *Comment. in Summa Theologica,* II–II, q. 148, art. 4.

91 L. Ferretti, *In honorem D. Thomae Aquinatis sexto saeculo exeunte a sanctorum caelitum honoribus ipsi decretis Documenta Pontificia miris artis operibus illustrata* (Romae, 1923), tab. XIII, p. 75.

92 Cf. M. Grabmann, *Introduction to the Study of the Summa Theologica of St. Thomas*, trans. John S. Zybura, Ph.D. (St. Louis: B. Herder, 1930). J. Mausbach, *Thomas von Aquin als Meister christlicher Sittenlehre* (Münster, 1925). O. Lottin, O.S.B., has done much toward a doctrinal and historical understanding of the Ethical and Moral Theology of St. Thomas through his discussions and researches, which now are being condensed into a three-volume work: *Psychologie et Morale aux XIIe et XIIIe sièles* (Louvain-Gembloux, 1942 ff.).

93 *Summa Theologica,* II–II, q. 166. M. Grabmann, "La conoscenza scientifica della verità sotto l'aspetto etico secondo S. Tommaso d'Aquino," *Rivista di filosofia neoscolastica,* 1942, pp. 139–151.

94 Cf. M. Grabmann, *Die Idee des Lebens in der Theologie des hl. Thomas von Aquin* (Paderborn, 1922).

95 R. Martin, O.P., "Le développement de la spiritualité dominicaine," *La vie spirituelle*, 1921, II, p. 357.

96 *Acta Sanctorum,* Martii, tom. I, p. 661.

97 Deurwerders, O.P., *Militia angelica divi Thomae Aquinatis* (Lovanii, 1659). H. M. Iweins, O.P., *Le cordon de Saint Thomas d'Aquin ou la milice angélique* (Louvain, 1893).

98 R. Garrigou-Lagrange, O.P., "La virginité consacrée à Dieu selon S. Thomas," *La vie spirituelle,* 10 (1920), pp. 533–550.

M. Grabmann, *Gedanken des hl. Thomas über Jungfräulichkeit und besckauliches Leben. Zam gooährigen Jubiläum der Abtei St. Walburg in Eichstätt,* Historische Beiträge herausgegeben von K. Reid (Paderborn, 1935), p. 102 ff.

99 *Quodl.,* III, a. 17, ad. 3.

100 In *IV Sent.,* d. 49, a. 5, a. 3, ad. 9.

101 *De Perfectione vitae spiritualis,* cap. 9.

102 *Acta Sanctorum,* Martii, tom. I, p. 712.

103 Denifle, O.P., *Chartularium Universatis Parisiensis,* 1, p. 634. A. Callebaut, O.F.M., "Jean Pecham, O.F.M., et l'Augustinisme," *Archivum Franciscanum Historicum,* 18 (1925), pp. 471–472.

104 L. Baur, "Die Form der wissenschaftlichen Kritik bei Thomas von Aquin," *Aus der Geisteswelt des Mittelalters. Festschrift Grabmann* (Münster, 1936), pp. 688–709.

105 *Constitutio: Sollicita et provida,* no. 24.

106 Bishop Thomas Esser, O.P., *D. Thomae Aquinatis Doctoris Angelici et scholarum catholicarum patroni monita et preces* (Paderborn, 1890). A.D. Sertillanges, O.P., *Prières de Saint Thomas d'Aquin* (Paris, 1920). Also E. Gilson, at the end of his work *The Philosophy of St. Thomas Aquinas*, pp. 359–361, shows how the prayers and poetry of St. Thomas mirror his inner life. He also cites R. De Gourmont, *Le Latin mystique* (Paris, 1913), pp. 274–275. [*Translator's note:* The translation of these prayers is taken from the beautiful little work *The Angel of Aquino*, translated and edited by the faculty of Saint Albertus College, Racine, Wisconsin.]

107 L. Lavaud, "Notes distinctives de la sainteté," p. 357 ff.

108 *Summa Theologica*, II–II, q. 145, art. 2.

109 A. Walz, *San Tommaso d'Aquino*, p. 177.

110 *Acta Sanctorum*, Martii, tom. I, p. 670.

111 Molkenboer, O.P., in: A.W. Winckel, O.P., en F. Van Goethen, S. *Thomas van Aquino,* pp. 166, 202.

112 J. A. Endres, "Ein Zyklus von Wandgemälden aus dem Leben des hl. Thomas von Aquin in der Dominikanerkirche zu Regensburg," *Christliche Kunst,* 1909, pp. 265–271.
113 *In Ep. ad Coloss., c.* 2, lect. 1.
114 Cf. M. Grabmann, "Die Bewertung der weltlichen Wissenschaften bei Thomas von Aquin," *Philosophisches Jahrbuch,* 1924, 4. Heft.
115 P. Mandonnet, O.P., *Siger de Brabant et l'Averroisme latin au XIIIe siècle,* I (Louvain, 1911), p. 109.
116 S. Augustinus, In *Joann.,* tract. 13, n. 4.
117 *Compendium Theologiae,* cap. 2.
118 H. Denifle, O.P., *Deutsche Schriften des seligen Heinrich Seuse* (München, 1876), p. 315. K. Bihlmeyer, *Heinrich Seuse, Deutsche Schriften* (Stuttgart, 1907), p. 203.
119 M. Grabmann, "Der Benediktiner mystiker Johannes von Kastl, der Verfasser des Büchleins De adhaerendo Deo," *Theol. Quartalschrift,* 1920, p. 225 ff. D. J. Huyben, O.S.B., *Jean de Castl, De l'Union avec Dieu,* Saint-Maximin, 1923.
120 A. Touron, O.P., *La vie de S. Thomas,* p. 420 f.
121 *In Ep. ad Galat.,* cap. 6, lect. 4.
122 *Summa Theologica,* II–II, q. 82, art. 3, ad. 2.
123 C. de Schäzler, *Introductio in* S. *Theologiam dogmaticam ad mentem* D. *Thomas Aquinatis* (Ratisbonae, 1882), p. 372.
124 *De perfectione vitae spiritualis*, cap. 10.
125 These treatises are taken from my publication: "Die kleineren Schriften des hl. Thomas von Aquin in ihrer Bedeutung für das geistliche Leben," *Linzer Theol. Quartalschrift,* 1923, pp. 645–658.
126 M. Grabmann, "Die Schrift De rationibus fidei contra Saracenos, Graecos et Armenos ad Cantorem Antiochenum des hl. Thomas von Aquin," *Scholastik,* 17 (1942), pp. 187–216.
127 Fr. Salvatore, *Due sermoni inediti de S. Tommaso d'Aquino* (Roma, 1912).

About the Author

Msgr. Martin Grabmann, Ph.D., was a German Roman Catholic priest, medievalist, and historian of theology and philosophy. He was a pioneer of the history of medieval philosophy and has been called "the greatest Catholic scholar of his time."

Sophia Institute

Sophia Institute is a nonprofit institution that seeks to nurture the spiritual, moral, and cultural life of souls and to spread the gospel of Christ in conformity with the authentic teachings of the Roman Catholic Church.

Sophia Institute Press fulfills this mission by offering translations, reprints, and new publications that afford readers a rich source of the enduring wisdom of mankind.

Sophia Institute also operates the popular online resource CatholicExchange.com. *Catholic Exchange* provides world news from a Catholic perspective as well as daily devotionals and articles that will help readers to grow in holiness and live a life consistent with the teachings of the Church.

In 2013, Sophia Institute launched Sophia Institute for Teachers to renew and rebuild Catholic culture through service to Catholic education. With the goal of nurturing the spiritual, moral, and cultural life of souls, and an abiding respect for the role and work of teachers, we strive to provide materials and programs that are at once enlightening to the mind and ennobling to the heart; faithful and complete, as well as useful and practical.

Sophia Institute gratefully recognizes the Solidarity Association for preserving and encouraging the growth of our apostolate over the course of many years. Without their generous and timely support, this book would not be in your hands.

www.SophiaInstitute.com
www.CatholicExchange.com
www.SophiaInstituteforTeachers.org